Marketing Channels: Structure and Strategy

Marketing Channels: Structure and Strategy

Edwin H. Lewis

Professor of Marketing
University of Minnesota

McGraw-Hill
Book Company
New York
St. Louis
San Francisco
Toronto
London
Sydney

Editors' Preface

The literature on distribution channels is large and diverse. While most marketing textbooks focus some attention on the institutional and managerial aspects of distribution channels, there are very few books devoted exclusively to this important and dynamic subject matter. Consistent with the objectives of the "Perspectives in Marketing" series, this book provides a contemporary and intensive treatment of an important area of marketing. In providing an integrated discussion of distribution channels by a highly respected scholar of the subject, we hope that this book will be useful both as a guide to those who are concerned with planning and decision making and as a supplementary textbook for a variety of marketing courses where there is a need for a more comprehensive discussion of channels than the basic textbook provides.

This book integrates theoretical and historical perspectives of distribution channels with those managerial problems in marketing which rest heavily upon channel considerations. The style of the book is largely analytical, and descriptive statistical detail of institutions is minimal. The analytical framework of the book provides a basis for understanding and evaluating channel relationships and institutions from both a societal and a managerial point of view.

Distribution channels reflect the society and the economy they serve. As society changes, so do distribution channels. The evolution of institutions and institutional relationships is therefore strongly related to economic development. The development of marketing institutions in the United States in the nineteenth and twentieth centuries affords a rich empirical basis for the application of theoretical concepts of institutional development and trade relationships. A number of the more important theoretical contributions by marketing scholars are outlined and discussed in this book and provide the basis for understanding the dynamics of distribution channel development. These same ideas are useful in a managerial context. With economic development continuing at home and abroad, channel changes and institutional evolution are inevitable. We think the ideas in this book will be useful in understanding and in anticipating these developments.

Robert D. Buzzell
Frank M. Bass

Preface

The literature covering marketing channels and their use is vast and scattered. It consists primarily of articles and chapters in principles of marketing texts which delineate the institutional structure of channels, sections of management-oriented marketing books which examine channel decisions, and a wide array of commodity studies which include channel material together with the other components of the marketing mix.

Also, through the years, a few students of marketing have offered explanations of marketing channels; and in recent years particularly there has been a steady flow of articles and monographs, plus an occasional book, which have thrown additional light on channel formation and channel relationships.

It would be difficult to review and synthesize all of the published work on channels in a book of this length, and the author has not attempted this task. He has tried to move in this direction, however, and has sought to do three things. First, the significant developments in channel evolution in this country are outlined, and some comparisons are made with developments in other parts of the world.

Second, distribution policies and channel decision-making processes are examined from the management viewpoint. In this connection, attention is given to the problems and conflicts which arise as the parties in the channel attempt to secure control of the channel network. Third, the concepts and theories which have been developed to explain marketing channels are presented.

It is hoped that this treatment will constitute a useful overview of marketing channels and of their development, dynamics, and management strategy. The author is indebted to many of those who have worked, as he has, in this particular vineyard; their names appear in the footnotes and in the Name Index.

Edwin H. Lewis

Contents

Editors' Preface   **v**

Preface   **vii**

Chapter 1   Functions and Dynamics of the Trade Channel   **1**

The Trade Channel   **2**

Channel Functions   **3**

Social Utility of Trade Channels   **4**

Dynamics of Trade Channels   **5**

The Channel in the Marketing Mix   **5**

Summary   **7**

Chapter 2   Evolution of Channels   **8**

The First Middlemen   **8**

Anglo-Saxon Trade   **9**

Markets and Fairs   **10**

Early Merchants   **11**

The Colonial Shipping Merchant   **12**

Jobbers and Merchant Wholesalers   **12**

Colonial Retailers   **16**

Growth of Large-scale Retailers   **16**

Threat to Wholesalers   **17**

A Case Study of Changes in Wholesaling   **19**

Wholesalers Carve Out New Niches   **20**

Status of Merchant Wholesalers   **21**

Limited-service Wholesalers   **24**

Manufacturers' Wholesale Branches   **25**

Agent Middlemen   **27**

Assemblers of Farm Products   **28**

The Changing Retail Structure   **28**
The Supermarket   **30**
The Discount House   **32**
The Wheel of Retailing   **33**
Countervailing Power   **36**
The Merchandise-Service Mix   **37**
Limitations to Innovation by Wholesalers and Retailers   **38**
Political Action and Channel Innovation   **40**

Chapter 3   Marketing Channels in Other Countries   **42**

British Marketing Structure   **44**
Retailing in Western Europe   **46**
Large-scale Retail Innovations   **48**
Impact of the European Common Market   **50**
Marketing behind the Iron Curtain   **51**
Changes in Wholesale Structures   **54**
Dominance of the Wholesaler in Japan   **55**
Marketing in Underdeveloped Countries   **57**

Chapter 4   Control of the Channel Network   **62**

Balance between Conflict and Cooperation in the Channel   **64**
Channel Conflicts   **64**
Methods of Securing Channel Control   **66**
Integration   **68**
Voluntary Chains   **70**
Channel Efficiency   **72**
Governmental Controls over Trade-channel Relationships   **73**
Exclusive Distribution Arrangements   **75**
Territorial Restrictions   **76**
Franchise Arrangements   **77**
Reciprocity   **79**

Chapter 5   Distribution Policies   **82**

Manufacturers' Distribution Policies   **83**
Direct Sale to Retailers   **84**
General versus Limited Distribution   **85**

Dual Distribution   88
Reciprocity   90
Wholesaler Distribution Policies   93
Voluntary Chains   94
Wholesale Trading Areas   97
Wholesale-Retail Buying Policies   100
Retail Buying Organizations   102
Distributor Brands   103
Policies of Industrial Buyers   104
Buying Policies of the Federal Government   106

Chapter 6   Channel Decisions   108

Channel Decisions as Part of Marketing Mix   108
Allocation of Functions among Units in the Channel   110
Manufacturer-Retailer Channel   110
Manufacturer-Consumer Channel   112
Manufacturer-Wholesaler Channel   112
Wholesaler-Retailer Relations   113
Qualitative Channel-decision Factors   115
The Product Line   115
Characteristics and Requirements of the Market   116
Capability of the Manufacturer   118
Competitive Practices   118
Suitability of Channels   120
Legal Restraints on Channel and Customer Selection   120
Quantitative Factors in Channel Selection   121
Time Factor in Channel Selection   123
Innovation and Channel Selection   124
Selection of Trade Customers   126
Factors Governing Selection of Outlets   127
Evaluation of Distribution Outlets   128
Need for Feedback from Distributor-Dealer Organization   129
Channel-decision Model   130
Quantitative Channel-decision Techniques   133

Chapter 7   Theoretical Explanations of Trade Channels   136

The Transvection Concept   139
Marketing Flows   140

Market Separation Theory	**141**
Depot Theory of Distribution	**142**
The Sorting Concept	**142**
Concept of Postponement	**144**
Conditions Underlying Need for Middlemen	**146**
Dynamics of Marketing Channels	**147**
Bibliography	**149**
Name Index	**169**
Subject Index	**171**

Marketing
Channels:
Structure
and
Strategy

1

Functions and Dynamics of the Trade Channel

Modern industrial societies have become increasingly complex in many respects. Not the least of these complexities is the economic structure and that part of it which is our particular concern, the trade structure. In a primitive culture very little, if any, trade exists. The family or tribal group is almost entirely self-sufficient. The group is composed of individuals who are both communal producers and consumers of whatever goods and services can be made available.

As economies evolve, people begin to specialize in some aspect of economic activity. They engage in agriculture, or fishing, or one of the basic crafts. As a result, they start to exchange or trade some of their output (and, eventually, a large share of it) for needed goods which have been produced by others. With this exchange, the first channels of distribution appear. They are, however, very simple channels and involve direct contact between two parties who are producers of one product and consumers of the other. This situation may be shown diagrammatically as follows:

Producer-Consumer ⇆ Producer-Consumer

With the growth of specialization, particularly industrial specialization, and with improvements in methods of transportation and communication, channels of distribution become longer and more complex. Cotton produced in Texas may be spun into thread and woven into cloth in New England, Great Britain, or Japan. Since cotton has a world market, trade channels must connect the grower in a specialized area of production with spinners around the world who for historical or market reasons are located where they are.

The Trade Channel

The purpose of a "trade channel" or "channel of distribution" (the terms are synonymous) is to bridge the gap between the producer of a product and the user of it, whether the parties are located in the same community or in different countries thousands of miles apart. When a housewife patronizes a local bakery, the trade channel is very short, in fact the shortest possible; the baker sells directly to the consumer. The housewife in this case is functioning as buying agent for the family, which is the consumption unit. This channel may be shown as follows:

Producer (Baker)→Consumer

On the same shopping trip, the housewife may visit a grocery store to purchase sugar. Even if the sugar refiner were located only a few miles away, the channel would be much more complex, typically:

Sugar Refiner→Sugar Broker→Grocery Wholesaler→Grocery Retailer→Consumer

or

Sugar Refiner→Sugar Broker→Grocery Chain→Consumer

If she also buys imported spices, they have probably moved through two or three crude-spice wholesalers in the country of origin plus perhaps an importer, a packer, a wholesaler, and a retailer of the packaged product in this country. The reasons for the varying makeup and complexity of trade channels will be discussed in later chapters.

The institutional components of trade channels fall into three categories: (1) the producer of the product—a craftsman, manufacturer, farmer, or other extractive-industry producer; (2) the user of the product—an individual or household, a business buyer, an institution, or government; and (3) certain middlemen at the wholesale and/or retail level.[1] Middlemen may or may not take title to the goods themselves, and they may or may not handle the goods physically, but they do perform the crucial function of facilitating the transfer of title.

The terminal points of a particular channel are the producer at the point of origin and the user at the point of consumption or final purchase. If a consumer product, such as an item of apparel, is traced back to the sources of the raw materials, several channels will be uncovered. There will be separate channels for the finished garment, the finished cloth from which the garment is made, the buttons and other materials incorporated in the garment, the unfinished cloth (i.e., cloth which needs to be bleached, dyed, or printed), the yarn, and the basic fiber (cotton, wool, silk, or synthetic).

When two or more manufacturing processes are integrated, as when one company spins the yarn, dyes it, and manufactures the finished cloth, the channels of distribution which existed when these operations were performed by separate firms are eliminated. In their place we simply have intracompany transfers, although quite possibly various company divisions or subsidiaries, or even plant locations, may be involved.

Channel Functions

In order to accomplish the transfer of goods from producer to consumer, a number of functions or activities need to be performed. These involve particularly the transfer of title (buying and selling); the physical movement of goods (transportation) accompanied by necessary storage; the search for markets or sources of supply (sales promotion on the selling side and certain aspects of purchasing on the other); and the payment for goods (financing). Other functions, depending on the classification one uses, may be added to the list.

As indicated above, the essential qualification for a participant in a channel of distribution is that he be involved in the transfer of title. Either he takes title himself, as do merchant wholesalers and retailers, or he acts in a sales or buying capacity as agent for a principal. Among the latter are brokers, commission houses, manufacturers' agents, and resident buying offices. The central function of all these institutions is buy-

---

[1] The term "middleman" refers to any agency in the channel engaged in buying and selling other than the producer or final buyer. The term incorporates both wholesale and retail establishments.

ing and/or selling. They may or may not perform additional services such as storage, financing, technical service, risk bearing, etc. Unless an organization is directly concerned with transferring title, however, it is not a part of the trade channel.

A very large number of businesses—transportation agencies, public warehouses, advertising agencies, advertising media, marketing research companies, and financial institutions—in some way facilitate the transfer of goods, but their services are of an auxiliary nature, and they are not included in the channel of distribution.

Social Utility of Trade Channels

As an economic mechanism, the primary function of a trade channel is to handle the flow of goods, especially the transfer of title from the producer of the goods to the individual or economic unit which is to use them. Consumers, whatever their type, want a particular package of goods and services. The services desired may include convenience, such as ease of shopping or delivery; some type of financing; the availability of parts and repair services; technical assistance in connection with purchase or use or both; wide merchandise selection; trial use or return privileges; rental with option to buy; attractive and comfortable surroundings in which to shop, etc.

To survive, a channel must not only provide the necessary mix of goods and services, it must supply them at a cost which is acceptable to the consumer. If a desired product is highly unique, is not available from alternative sources, and has no substitutes, the user may tolerate comparatively high channel costs. As alternatives become available, however, either with respect to goods or channels, comparative channel costs become increasingly important. In the purchase of staples, particularly food, the consumer is likely to purchase at the store which offers the lowest prices; and as will be shown in later chapters, the consumer is likely to display patronage loyalty only as long as a store's offerings are no less favorable than those of competitors.

Inherent in channel structure, therefore, is the factor of social efficiency. This takes the customary input-output form in which outputs represent the services received by the consumer and inputs constitute the channel functions performed and their respective costs. Although it is difficult to attach dollar figures to channel functions, particularly to services received, consumers do, in fact, undertake to make such subjective evaluations. They decide whether the services performed for them by the neighborhood grocer, for example, are worth the higher prices paid compared with those in a supermarket. The fact that mass merchandisers are taking a larger share of the food business seems to indicate that an increasing number of consumers would rather not pay for the independent grocer's services. Similarly, consumers compare the product-service mix of department stores and discount stores against their respective prices.

Dynamics of Trade Channels

The twin pressures to improve channel services and to reduce channel costs result in continuous changes in trade-channel patterns. These include changes both in channel composition and in the relative importance of alternative channels. All parties in the channel—original producer, wholesaler, retailer, and consumer—are constantly searching for more effective channel relationships. There is, consequently, a continuing state of flux in the allocation of channel functions. Functions are shifted among existing members; and some members may be dropped or "cut out" or perhaps replaced by others who have certain efficiencies to offer.

From day to day, channels may appear to the casual observer to be quite stable, but the forces of change are constantly at work, and the rewards of the free-enterprise system go to those who introduce more productive and efficient channel modifications. In some parts of the world, as indicated in Chapter 3, this is not necessarily true, and channels may exist without great change for generations. The history of marketing institutions in the United States, however, tells a different story. In our economy, there are very few protected channels or niches in a given channel. Competition for customers is relentless; this has brought about numerous evolutionary channel developments of the type discussed in Chapter 2.

The Channel in the Marketing Mix

As indicated above, trade channels under competitive conditions must meet the social-efficiency test. For manufactured products, a more pragmatic test is whether the channel fits the manufacturer's marketing strategy. Having first selected a market which he wants to cover, the manufacturer must then devise a marketing mix which will enable him to cultivate this market most effectively. The major components of the marketing mix are product line, packaging, sales promotion, price, services offered, and distribution channels. Policies are established within these areas, and specific decisions are made to implement them.

The manufacturer may have a choice of channels available to him, particularly if the company is large and the line is broad. In such cases, he may wish to take full responsibility for distribution and sell directly to the user, if industrial products are involved, or directly to the retailer, in the case of consumer goods.

Where the manufacturer is small and has a limited line, he may find it necessary to sell his entire output through agents, either because he lacks the know-how and/or financial resources to maintain his own sales organization or because an attempt to sell through the latter would be prohibitively expensive. If he is able to sell efficiently through his own salesmen but potential users are very numerous and spread over a wide area, he will probably find it necessary to sell through merchant wholesalers.

The characteristics of a firm's markets, the nature of its product line, and its own operating characteristics determine not only the range of channel choice but also the relative strength or status of the manufacturer in the channel compared with other channel members. Since the middle of the last century, particularly since World War I, dominant retail institutions such as chains, mail-order houses, and department stores have emerged and flourished. Quite frequently, they occupy a stronger position in the channel than their small suppliers. This often permits them to specify the conditions under which they will purchase, particularly when the store's own brands are used or where the manufacturer's brand is weak and relatively unknown to consumers.

Whenever large retailers, or major wholesalers, are in a position to dominate the channel, their marketing strategy thus becomes the controlling factor in the channel, particularly when alternative sources of supply are available.

Under certain conditions, channel control shifts all the way to the user. This occurs when the Federal government purchases products needed in the space program, for example, or when the sole canner or packer in an area purchases from nearby growers. Monopsony situations such as these favor the buyer against the seller.

On balance, the channel through which a given product unit will be sold depends on how the participants in the channel decide to share the channel responsibilities and with whom they choose to share them. These choices are not the prerogative of any particular member of the channel. Rather they are forged out, as it were, by the application of power tactics and pressures within the channel. The balance of power may shift as the parties gain or lose status through their own marketing mix. Furthermore, new types of middlemen emerge as opportunities for new kinds of specialization by product line, markets served, or functions performed appear. The factors which govern channel selection and which determine the allocation of distribution functions among members of the channel, which have been lightly touched here, will be discussed in detail in Chapters 4, 5, and 6.

Summary

Although the marketing structure of the United States is exceedingly complex, it is an organized complexity, not to be confused with either chaos or inefficiency. In the final analysis, each institution must prove its worth to the channel parties with whom it deals. All parties have varying degrees of choice, and in large measure they exercise freedom to choose. Most channels are highly competitive; this competition brings about new and better ways of accomplishing the job of product distribution.

Because of the inertia which may exist in some situations, and because a time lag occurs before the need for change may be recognized, it is undoubtedly true that the overall system never reaches a point of optimum social efficiency. However, our channel system has shown constant change and improvement, and there is every indication that these changes will continue, with no slackening in the pace.

2

Evolution of Channels

The history of man is a progression from hunter to herder to agriculturist to craftsman. The first trade occurred when someone needed food or craftwork produced by someone else and had a product that he could part with in exchange. The earliest transactions were simple and direct, between two parties who needed something for their own consumption.

The First Middlemen

The first middlemen were merchants or traders who moved high-value products over the caravan routes of the Mediterranean world or across the great Sea itself. This trade probably existed prior to the use of written records. By 1500 B.C., the Phoenicians had developed an active sea trade. During the centuries of their ascendancy, they traded all over the Mediterranean and, passing through Gibraltar, visited what are now England and the western part of Africa.

Such trade, however, supplied only a very small share of the products needed by the early civilizations. For example, "The Egyptians were not a commercial people. Their main resource was agriculture, and though they developed some of the industrial arts to great efficiency, they used the products for direct consumption rather than for trade." [1] The products traded in this era were primarily luxury goods—ivory, precious woods, wine, oil, gold, linen, metalwares, etc. The lives of most people were seldom touched by this trade, and they remained locked in their self-sufficient economies.

[1] Clive Day, *A History of Commerce,* Longmans, Green & Co., Inc., New York, 1926, p. 9. By permission of David McKay Company, Inc.

As new civilizations grew around the Mediterranean, the volume of trade increased and the structure of distribution became more complex. It could be said of the Athenian economy:

> Trade, not in industry or finance, is the soul of the Athenian economy. Though many producers still sell directly to the consumer, a growing number of them require the intermediary of the market, whose function it is to buy and store goods until the consumer is ready to purchase them. In this way a class of retailers arises, who peddle their wares through the streets or in the wake of armies, or at festivals or fairs, or offer them for sale in shops or stalls in the agora or elsewhere in the town.[2]

Following the conquest of Greece the center of commerce shifted to Rome, where:

> The improvement of government and transport expanded Mediterranean trade to an unprecedented amplitude. At one end of the busy process of exchange were peddlers hawking through the countryside everything from sulphur matches to costly imported silks; wandering auctioneers who served also as town criers and advertised lost goods and runaway slaves; daily markets and periodical fairs; shopkeepers haggling with customers, cheating with false or tipped scales, and keeping a tangential eye for the aedile's inspectors of weights and measures. A little higher in the commercial hierarchy were shops that manufactured their own merchandise; these were the backbone of both industry and trade. At or near the port were wholesalers who sold, to retailers or consumers, goods recently brought in from abroad; sometimes the owner or captain of a vessel would sell his cargo directly from the deck.[3]

Anglo-Saxon Trade

After the decline of the Roman Empire, European civilization, especially on the outer fringes, retrogressed to a more primitive state, and trade had to evolve once again. In the British Isles, for example, during the early medieval period, the Anglo-Saxon economy was agricultural, with each family group or manorial village dependent almost entirely on its own production. Food was produced locally, which resulted typically in either shortages or surpluses. Houses were made from local materials, and clothing was made from wool and flax produced in the area.

---

[2] A. Zimmern, *The Greek Commonwealth,* 4th ed., Oxford University Press, Fair Lawn, N.J., 1924, p. 283.

[3] Will Durant, *The Story of Civilization: Part III, Caesar and Christ,* Simon and Schuster, Inc., New York, 1944, p. 328. Copyright, 1944, by Will Durant. Reprinted by permission of the publisher.

A very few products were secured from the outside—salt, iron, millstones, and tar, to name some of the most important. "These wares were essential to existence; by channels so obscure that they cannot now be traced they reached the places where they were wanted and were purchased with part of the manor's scanty surplus." [4]

Occupational specialization gradually developed, starting with the smith; later, others whose occupational surnames have carried down to the present day appeared: miller, baker, thatcher, tyler, cooper, etc. These craftsmen produced not for stock but on order, in accordance with the user's requirements. Consequently, they were producer specialists, not merchants.

The earliest middleman in what we would now term "domestic marketing" was a traveling pack peddler called a "chapman." He generally originated in one of the seaport towns and with the consent of the local ruler or king traveled through the hinterland, where he was in danger of being robbed and was universally treated with suspicion.[5]

Travel over long distances was expensive, and most goods moved within a limited area, but by the tenth century merchants were operating regularly between the British Isles and the Continent.

According to Day, the merchant of the period around 1000 A.D.

> . . . was not the specialist that he afterwards became, but was a jack-of-all-trades. He might be wholesaler and retailer, transporter and peddler, and often an artisan too. Nothing like the country store of the present day existed, and trade outside the few centers where markets had been established was carried on by peddlers, who carried their wares on the back or on a pack animal. Every merchant was sure to be something of a soldier, as he was thrown largely on his own resources for self-defense; and he often assumed the garb of a missionary or pilgrim to get the help of the church in carrying on his trade. The pilgrim was exempt from many burdens laid on the ordinary traveler or merchant, and though this exemption had later to be abolished, because it was so frequently abused, it seems to have been of great use in helping commerce through its early stages.[6]

Markets and Fairs

During the latter part of the Anglo-Saxon period, two trade institutions developed, the market and the fair. The first markets were simple

[4] Day, *op. cit.*, p. 37.

[5] George B. Hotchkiss, *Milestones of Marketing,* The Macmillan Company, New York, 1938, p. 9.

[6] Day, *op. cit.*, p. 39.

meeting places at which people met to trade at designated times (usually one day a week) under the protection of the church or a feudal lord. In some instances, booths were set up in churchyards for trade after Sunday services.

It became customary for those engaged in trade to pay a toll for protection; in addition, other charges frequently were levied for the use of stalls and weighing facilities, for crossing bridges, etc. These taxes led to attempts at evasion (forestalling) through selling outside the established market facilities. Consequently, after the Norman conquest, markets were more closely controlled and trade more closely regulated.

The fair originated in the church festival, and each fair came to be an annual event of perhaps several days' duration, centered on a particular saint's day.

One of the basic concepts of medieval trade (other than limiting trade to specified markets) was that *direct* trade between producer and user was to be desired. Consequently, there were heavy penalties for "regrating" (buying and selling again in the same market) and "engrossing" (buying larger quantities than needed for one's own use).

Early Merchants

As time went on, particularly after development of the craft guilds, direct trade proved inadequate, and the position of the small retailer evolved.

> The petty shopkeeper stood a step above the peddler. He had a regular shop in town, where he displayed his wares, and often went on trips to the markets of other towns, where he set up a booth and carried on such trade as the town regulations allowed.
>
> Still another step above the shopkeeper was the real merchant who had his warehouse from which he supplied the retail traders, and who bought up considerable quantities of goods at the great fairs at home and abroad. It is doubtful whether we can find in this class in northern Europe any men who devoted themselves entirely to wholesale trade; and merchants had not yet specialized so that each would devote himself exclusively to the trade in a particular ware. . . . Vicko von Geldersen was a draper of Hamburg. . . . He imported cloth wholesale and sold it both wholesale and retail. But he made use of his connection with Bruges, which was the great cloth market, to send there for sale iron, honey, meat, butter, etc., and to import such wares as oil, spices, figs, and almonds, which he sold to smaller dealers in many cities of Germany.[7]

[7] *Ibid.*, p. 113.

By the end of the Middle Ages merchants who traded only at wholesale had developed, and we also find the beginnings of the commission merchant, or factor. Some of the latter bought and sold on their own account, also, and sometimes specialized by commodity line.[8]

The Colonial Shipping Merchant

During the early years of the American colonies, the leading merchants performed functions closely related to those of European merchants of an earlier day. Jones describes the activities of one such "shipping merchant":

> John Hull (1624–83), famous mintmaster of Massachusetts, was the first American merchant of consequence. Hull's business was of a varied and general nature. From farmers, artisans, traders, and fishermen he obtained by barter such commodities as stoves, casks, wheat, port, fish, and furs. These he sent to Virginia, the West Indies, or England and obtained in return lead, shot, gunpowder, sugar, liquor, and dry goods. The ships in which he sent his cargoes were either entirely owned by him or he owned a sizeable share in them. . . .
>
> The merchants of Hull's time could not confine themselves strictly to a wholesale business. Their account books show that they often sold at retail. The wants of the colonists were too often satisfied by labor in the shop, in the home, or on the farm to enable a strictly wholesale business to exist.[9]

Jobbers and Merchant Wholesalers

By the beginning of the nineteenth century, the jobber had made his appearance, buying from import merchants in the Atlantic Seaboard cities (since most goods were imported) and selling to retailers. The first half of this century also saw the rise of the commission merchant, or factor, who was particularly important in dealing with agricultural products such as cotton and tobacco but also handled the sale of manufactured goods as well.

Merchant wholesalers commonly conducted a commission business, handling goods on consignment, as well as buying and selling in their own name. In their dealings with country stores, wholesalers often

[8] *Ibid.*, p. 142.
[9] Fred M. Jones, "The Development of Marketing Channels in the United States to 1920," in Richard M. Clewett (ed.), *Marketing Channels,* Richard D. Irwin, Inc., Homewood, Ill., 1954, p. 36.

found it desirable to handle on a commission basis the agricultural products the store had assembled. This strengthened the wholesaler's ties with these retailers and facilitated the sale of merchandise to them.

It was also common for wholesale merchants to conduct a retail business; this continued until rising wholesale volume after the Civil War made it economical to specialize in wholesaling. Prior to the Civil War, wholesalers handled both domestic goods and goods which they imported. In fact, importing was a major wholesale function during this period.

Another function sometimes combined with wholesaling was manufacturing. The nineteenth-century wholesaler, therefore, often conducted a multiple business, combining jobbing of domestic lines with importing, combining factoring with a merchant business, or combining wholesaling with retailing or manufacturing—and sometimes combining all three. With the growth of the country after the Civil War, the wholesaler tended to specialize in domestic or foreign goods, in a merchant or commission business, and to divest himself of the retail business.

The term "jobber" has suffered from ambiguity. Originally, it was used by firms who bought merchandise from importers in original packages and then resold in smaller quantities to retailers. As time went on, virtually the same functions were performed by importers and merchant wholesalers. Some wholesalers have continued to refer to themselves as jobbers, but the term has come to be synonymous with full-service merchant wholesalers.

By the mid 1800s, agent middlemen were well established. In addition to the commission merchant, or factor, there were manufacturers' agents, selling agents, and brokers. These middlemen were not the specialized middlemen which they have since become. "Any agent was likely to be called a commission merchant, and any firm might conduct more than one kind of agent wholesaler business." [10]

The common characteristic of agent middlemen is that they do not take title. Some handle the merchandise physically. Others do not. All participate in buying and selling activities on a commission or fee basis. Table 1 outlines the current functions and operations of agent middlemen.

[10] *Ibid.*, p. 49.

TABLE 1

Operating Characteristics of Agent Middlemen

Type of agent	Handle goods physically	Channel relationships	Services performed	Operating expenses* (percent of sales)	Major commodity fields
Auction company	Yes	Represents seller; this relationship not necessarily continuous	Receives merchandise and prepares for sale, displays samples, prepares sales catalog, provides auction facilities for quick sale, transmits net proceeds to seller	2.5	Raw tobacco, fruit, furs
Broker†	No	Represents buyer or seller, usually on a free-lance basis	Serves as go-between in negotiating a sale; may operate under price restrictions	1.9 (represents buyer) 2.4 (represents seller)	Various products, particularly raw materials
Commission house or merchant	Yes	Represents seller; basically free-lance but tends to establish continuing contacts with shippers	Receives consignments, stores and displays, negotiates sales, remits net proceeds to shipper, may extend credit to buyer	2.2	Agricultural products: fresh produce, grain, livestock
Manufacturers' agent or representative	Some carry stocks	Represents seller in specified geographical area on a contractual basis; usually handles allied but noncompeting lines	Takes full sales responsibility in assigned area; may operate under price restrictions	5.9	Many lines of manufactured goods: textiles and apparel, food products, automotive, sporting goods, hardware,

Selling agent	Usually not	Generally takes full responsibility under contract for sale of principal's entire output; his control over price varies; usually handles allied and sometimes competing lines	Performs all services a manufacturer's sales organization normally would perform; may give financial and technical assistance to manufacturer, including product design	3.5	Very important in textiles, dry goods, and apparel; also in house furnishings and industrial supplies and equipment
Purchasing agent	No	Buys for wholesalers or large retailers	Purchases for clients located in outlying areas, maintains contact with central market sellers	2.7	Hardware, electrical equipment, industrial lines
Resident‡ Buyer	No	Purchases in central markets for outlying department and specialty stores	Purchases for client stores as ordered. aids store buyers, furnishes market information and advice		Apparel and other department store lines

*Expense data from 1958 Census of Business, Wholesale Trade, United States Summary. Comparable data not shown in the 1963 Census of Business.

†The food broker is of considerable importance in the grocery field. However, his operations are essentially those of a manufacturers' agent.

‡In addition to independent resident buyers, there are several major cooperative buying organizations owned by retailers. These organizations offer a wide range of services. They buy staples in large quantities, develop private labels, maintain display and buyer service facilities, devise promotional programs, and facilitate the exchange of operating information among their members. Members are department and specialty stores, ordinarily only one in a city.

Colonial Retailers

Sales at retail in the seaboard cities of the American colonies were made by combined wholesale-retail enterprises, by the specialty shops which gradually appeared, and by craftsmen who operated their own establishments and sold their own output. In these cities, the public market was an important source of food products.

Residents in rural areas, particularly those on the frontier, had to depend on general stores and the traveling peddler. The general store served both as retail outlet and as assembler (i.e., local wholesaler) of furs and farm products.

The peddlers were of several kinds:

> Some of the original peddlers were themselves the manufacturers of the goods they carried. The early Connecticut clock-makers would go out on horseback with a few clocks and sell them directly to the consumer. . . . The Berlin makers of tinware would make up a stock, load it in two baskets on a horse and then go out to sell it through the countryside. Subsequently, they hired others to do the peddling from covered carts. These peddlers are said to have reached all parts of the country. In his final development, the tin peddler was a middleman with a varied stock of all sorts of articles. The flat-boat peddler was a somewhat similar phenomenon who flourished on the Mississippi River for quite a period.[11]

Specialty shops, unless they produced their own wares, purchased from shipping merchants, importers, or domestic manufacturers. Jobbers or wholesalers also supplied the general stores and peddlers. As the population moved westward, some of the general stores evolved into wholesalers and carried on a joint wholesale-retail business.

Growth of Large-scale Retailers

In the first half of the nineteenth century, the forerunners of the present-day department store and chain store were established. Together with the mail-order house, these came to be known as large-scale retailers. The Civil War was a turning point in American retailing; the major growth in large-scale retailing occurred after the war.

It is difficult to state when the first department store appeared in this country. Retail enterprises which later became nationally known department stores were established in the mid 1800s, but in their early years

---

[11] Hotchkiss, *op. cit.*, p. 164.

and may carry oil-well equipment, welding supplies, valves and fittings, power-transmission equipment, mechanical rubber goods, abrasives, etc.

In the past, manufacturers frequently have been dissatisfied with the kind of coverage and service they have received from the older general-line wholesaler who attempted to sell to all types of users in his trading area. The newer, more efficiently operated specialty wholesalers have a high competence in a limited market and are better able to give manufacturers the kind of service they require.

Status of Merchant Wholesalers

The net result of the shifting position of the merchant wholesaler in various commodity fields is that, on balance, the importance of merchant wholesalers seems not to have greatly changed over the years, although satisfactory data to support this assertion are difficult to obtain.

The longest available series of data for wholesalers is that prepared by Prof. Harold Barger and shown in Table 2. These figures refer to the "value added" by wholesalers—the difference between the purchase and sales prices of goods handled by wholesalers. Barger's data include only those goods eventually sold by retailers and thus exclude sales of wholesalers to business users, institutions, and governments. Professor Cox believes that the Barger figure for 1948 is probably too high and that the wholesaler's share may have decreased in recent decades.[16]

TABLE 2

Market Value Added by Distribution for All Commodities Marketed through Retailers, 1869–1948 (Percent of Retail Value)

Value added by:	1869	1879	1889	1899	1909	1919	1929	1929	1939	1948
Wholesalers	9.5	9.6	9.6	9.2	8.9	8.5	8.1	8.0	7.6	7.7
Retailers	23.2	24.1	25.1	26.2	27.6	28.0	28.9	28.6	29.7	29.7
Wholesalers and retailers	32.7	33.7	34.7	35.4	36.5	36.5	37.0	36.6	37.3	37.4

Source: Harold Barger, *Distribution's Place in the American Economy since 1869,* Princeton University Press, Princeton, New Jersey, 1955, pp. 57, 60. The three columns to the right are shown separately because they are based on different data, particularly the United States censuses of business, which were first taken in 1929.

[16] Reavis Cox, C. S. Goodman, and T. C. Fichandler, *Distribution in a High-level Economy,* Prentice-Hall, Inc., Englewood Cliffs, N.J., 1965, p. 158.

Sales of merchant wholesalers may be compared with trade and manufacturers' sales. Though these data are available for a limited period, they show a high degree of stability, as indicated in Table 3.

TABLE 3

Sales of Merchant Wholesalers Related to Total Sales in Manufacturing and Trade

	Total manufacturing and trade	Merchant wholesalers	Percent of total
1939	$133.4 billion	$ 21.8 billion	16.4
1948	437.3	76.5	17.5
1954	567.7	101.0	17.7
1958	648.2	115.6	17.8
1962	769.3	134.2	17.4
1963	803.5	140.0	17.4

Source: John M. Brion, *Marketing through the Wholesaler-Distributor Channel,* no. 10, Marketing for Executives series, American Marketing Association, Chicago, 1965, p. 53.

In a study of the channels of distribution for industrial products, it was found that such changes as have occurred in channels for this type of product, since World War II, involved the *addition* of the industrial distributor, not his elimination.[17]

The period since World War II has demonstrated that wholesaling is still a very vital marketing activity and that the independent wholesaler is a necessary part of the channel of distribution. Between 1948 and 1963, the sales of retail establishments increased approximately 80 percent, whereas sales of merchant wholesalers increased 98 percent.[18] The strength of the independent wholesaler may be seen in several consumer goods areas where wholesalers historically have been important but where it was believed that they were losing ground. Wholesalers of grocery products, hardware, furniture, drugs, electrical appliances, confectionery, footwear, and jewelry have had greater increases in sales in

[17] William T. Diamond, *Distribution Channels for Industrial Goods,* Bureau of Business Research Monograph No. 114, Ohio State University Press, Columbus, Ohio, 1963, p. 69.

[18] U.S. Department of Commerce, Bureau of the Census, *Census of Business,* wholesale and retail trades, 1948 and 1963. Data in this section are calculated from the United States summaries.

they operated as dry-goods stores or apparel stores. As their sales grew, other lines were added and, in time, were organized into departments.

R. H. Macy & Company, Inc., was founded by Captain R. H. Macy in 1858, and dealt exclusively in fancy goods. Five years later, it introduced millinery. In 1861, John Wanamaker was opened as a men's clothing store in Philadelphia, Pennsylvania. In 1877, the store was arranged into sixteen departments. In 1851, Jordan Marsh Company was opened in Boston, Massachusetts, as a dry goods jobbing house and was expanded ten years later into a large retail store. Gladding Dry Goods Company, of Providence, Rhode Island, was established in 1866, and four years later was known as the largest and best dry-goods store in Providence. Gimbel Brothers owes its origin to a small store started in 1842 in Vincennes, Indiana. Adam Gimbel, the founder, made a specialty of trading furs and produce for dry goods. . . . Lord and Taylor opened in 1826 on Catherine Street, New York City. Arnold Constable was first established in 1827 on Front Street, New York City, and made two other moves before reaching its present location in 1915. The A. T. Stewart building was constructed to house a department store which opened early in 1863. As to which was the first actual department store, the decision would seem to rest between Jordan Marsh and Company and A. T. Stewart.[12]

The post-Civil War period saw the establishment of the two largest general-mail-order houses, Montgomery Ward in 1872 and Sears Roebuck in 1886. During the last decades of the nineteenth century and the early years of the twentieth, these two houses blanketed the rural areas of the country. Despite strong opposition from local stores, jobbers, and newspapers, the large general-mail-order houses thrived and over the intervening decades have become a classic example of adaptation to changing times.

The large, modern-day chain dates back to 1859 with the establishment of the first store of what is now the Great Atlantic and Pacific Tea Company, although the company was not incorporated until 1901. The first major variety chain, F. W. Woolworth Company, was started in 1879; and the early shoe chains—Melville, Florsheim, Kinney, and Endicott-Johnson—were founded in the mid 1890s.

Threat to Wholesalers

The development of large-scale retailers posed a major threat to the jobber and the merchant wholesaler. These retailers were large enough

[12] Norris A. Brisco, *Retailing,* 2d ed., Prentice-Hall, Inc., New York, 1947, p. 5. Copyright, 1947, Prentice-Hall, Inc.

to buy directly from manufacturers and so cut the wholesaler out of the channel. At the same time, some large multiline manufacturers found that they could sell directly to retailers by establishing their own wholesale branches. Caught within this pincer movement, wholesalers of finished consumer goods, it appeared, might be forced to abandon large segments of the market.

Actually, in some commodity fields the merchant wholesaler did decline substantially in importance. The general-merchandise wholesaler, one of the earliest types of wholesalers, went out of business with the small general-merchandise store. The major general-line retail institutions today are the department store, which buys almost entirely from manufacturers, and the variety store, of which more than 90 percent have been of the chain-store type.

The rise of department stores and soft-goods chains posed such a threat to the general-line dry-goods wholesaler that in some markets he also has virtually disappeared. Those who have survived have done so by shifting to a specialty wholesale operation involving franchised lines for key products and the use of private brands.

Most shoes are sold either by chains of shoe stores (some manufacturer-owned) or leased departments, or through independently operated specialty stores which are part of a manufacturer's franchised distribution system. The wholesaler has not been needed in these channels. Nevertheless, the growing diversification of footwear lines has resulted in greater use being made of the wholesaler.

In the convenience-goods fields, especially in groceries and hardware, the wholesaler frequently has ceased to operate as the supplier of independent retailers and, instead, sponsors one or more voluntary chains. Also, in drugs and to a lesser extent in groceries, retailers in many cities have established retailer cooperatives. In the grocery field particularly, an increasingly large share of the wholesale business is handled by voluntary-group cooperatives and retailer cooperatives. In 1948, voluntary-group cooperatives accounted for 27½ percent of the general-line wholesale grocery business, and retailer cooperatives had 10 percent. In 1963, the voluntary groups had 45 percent and the retailer cooperatives 25 percent, or 70 percent of the grocery business taken together.

This trend in the growth of cooperatives will, in all probability, continue. Frequently, cooperative groups have proved more than a match for the centrally owned grocery chains and have become the strongest located some distance from regular wholesalers. They issue catalogs or lists of available merchandise. These wholesalers have never been very important, and with the growing decentralization of wholesale establishments there will be less need for them. However, some who feature special lots of merchandise or special prices may continue to serve certain segments of the market.

Retailer-cooperative warehouses are sometimes included in the limited-function wholesaler category, as are rack jobbers. Since the latter handle nonfood items in supermarkets, by setting up and maintaining racks of merchandise which are placed in the store on a consignment basis, they are actually a type of specialty wholesaler.

The Bureau of the Census has not consistently tabulated data for limited-function wholesalers. However, the available data indicate that truck distributors increased in importance between 1948 and 1958 but declined both in numbers and in sales between 1958 and 1963. The growth of voluntary groups probably has restricted the market for truck distributors in the food field. Drop shippers have had a declining share of lumber-millwork sales in the postwar period. In 1948, they had 36 percent of this business. By 1963, this had dropped to 28 percent. During the decade 1948–1958, drop shippers in the coal industry increased their share of the wholesale coal business from 71 to 92 percent.[19]

Manufacturers' Wholesale Branches

In many commodity lines, manufacturers have established their own wholesale branches which carry stocks. These are particularly important in automobiles, electrical supplies, industrial chemicals, grocery products, industrial equipment, meat, drugs, farm machinery, and electrical appliances. Sales of these establishments have been about 15 percent of total sales of wholesalers since World War II.

Manufacturers' stock-carrying branches have been established in areas where the volume of sales warrants them and where either the manufacturer has become dissatisfied with wholesalers—particularly with respect to promotion—or the wholesalers have not been equipped to perform the specialized services desired. Unless the manufacturer has a wide line, or his products have high unit value, it is not likely that he

[19] Calculated from *Census of Business, Wholesale Trade, United States Summary,* 1948, 1958, and 1963.

can perform the wholesale functions at lower cost than the independent wholesaler.

Since World War II, sales of manufacturers' branches which carry stocks have increased faster than sales of merchant wholesalers in several commodity fields, as indicated in Table 5.

TABLE 5

Percentage Increase in Sales of Manufacturers' Stock-carrying Branches Compared with Merchant Wholesalers, 1948–1963

Commodity field	Manufacturers' sales branches (with stocks)	Merchant wholesalers
Construction, mining machinery	525	232
Lumber, millwork	520	103
Printing and writing paper, wrapping and other coarse paper	500	119
Amusement, sporting goods	366	260
Commercial and industrial machinery and equipment	343	65
Drugs	322	165
Electrical appliances	316	180
Footwear	278	94
Hardware	150	26
Paint	66	58

Source: *Census of Business, Wholesale Trade, United States Summary,* 1948 and 1963. Percentages calculated by the author.

For some product categories—meat, confectionery, dry goods, plumbing, heating and air-conditioning equipment and supplies, and service-establishment equipment—the dollar sales of manufacturers' branches actually declined substantially over the fifteen-year period.

Not all manufacturers' branches displace independent wholesalers. Some branches are actually regional warehouses which carry backup stocks on which wholesalers as well as other customers draw.

Operating costs of branches with stocks were 10.6 percent of sales in 1963 compared with 13.5 percent for merchant wholesalers, and a comparison of costs on a product-line basis indicates that net costs of branches, as reported in the *Census of Business,* are generally lower grocery establishments in their area. Between 1948 and 1963, the expense-to-sales ratio of voluntary grocery chains declined from 8.3 to 6.2 percent. The expense ratio of retailer cooperatives held constant at about 4.5 percent, while expenses of unaffiliated wholesale grocers increased from 8.7 to 9.2 percent.[13]

In order to consolidate their position and to secure control over good retail locations, cooperatives, especially of the voluntary type, have given increasing help to retailers in securing leases and in financing the new business. In some cases, the cooperatives either have established the stores themselves and run them until a good prospect appeared, or they have engaged in partial ownership of the stores. These practices, undoubtedly, will be continued.

A Case Study of Changes in Wholesaling

The changing character of grocery wholesaling has been portrayed in a study of the Los Angeles market during the period 1920–1946.[14] In 1920, three types of grocery wholesalers were operating in this market, (1) the full-line, full-service firm, (2) the limited-line, full-service wholesaler, and (3) wholesalers who served specialized markets such as restaurants and hotels. Although grocery chains maintained their own warehouses and handled about one-seventh of retail grocery sales, their purchases were made through wholesalers rather than direct from manufacturers.

During the years following World War I, the chains sought to purchase direct from manufacturers at discounts comparable to those given to wholesalers. Retailer cooperatives were established for the same purpose. The association of wholesale grocers actively opposed these moves by a threat of boycott against manufacturers who sold direct. The Federal Trade Commission (FTC) supported the retailers, however, by issuing a cease and desist order against the wholesalers which was later upheld in Federal court. In the resulting competition between the older wholesaler channel and the newer direct-to-retailer channel, only seven of the original sixteen grocery wholesalers survived. However, several

[13] For sales and expense data see U.S. Department of Commerce, Bureau of the Census, *Census of Business, Wholesale Trade, United States Summary,* 1948 and 1963.

[14] Ralph Cassady, Jr., and Wylie L. Jones, *The Changing Competitive Structure in the Wholesale Grocery Trade,* University of California Press, Berkeley, Calif., 1949.

new wholesale establishments came into being, including cash-and-carry operations and a truck distributor. By 1946, the remaining full-line, full-service establishments were handling only 15 percent of the volume, compared with 85 percent for this class in 1920. The bulk of the business was handled by retailer cooperatives, chain warehouses which purchased direct, and manufacturers' wholesale branches. These latter channels, which were not in existence in this market in 1920, had two-thirds of the grocery volume at the end of World War II.

Wholesalers Carve out New Niches

Wholesalers in some fields (automotive parts, for example) have increased in importance. Furthermore, new types of specialized wholesalers have appeared in some commodities. As a case in point, specialty pharmaceutical houses which concentrate on prescription items and offer multiple daily deliveries to their customers are found in some cities. Such service makes it possible for the druggist to reduce or eliminate inventories of slow-moving drugs.

Also in metropolitan areas, furniture wholesalers (a product line ordinarily bought directly from manufacturers) have emerged for the primary purpose of carrying backup stocks for department and furniture stores. These retailers, consequently, can supply customers who have special needs without carrying such items in stock.

Other examples of wholesalers who have evolved to perform special services or to meet the needs of specific market segments may be found in the industrial electrical field. These include limited-line "brokerage" houses, which use price appeal and sell fast-turn items by mail or telephone to customers located in distant markets, and a mail-order wholesaler who sells to customers located in smaller towns some distance from electrical distributors. Most electrical distributors handle a full line and sell to several types of customers, but some are highly specialized and cater to such specific markets as small residential electrical contractors, industrial or commercial contractors, industrial accounts, electric-sign manufacturers, or the marine market. By line, they may specialize in wire and cable, electrical repair parts, or lighting fixtures.[15]

Industrial distributors, likewise, may specialize by line and market

[15] Edwin H. Lewis, *Marketing Electrical Apparatus and Supplies,* McGraw-Hill Book Company, New York, 1961.

than for corresponding merchant wholesalers. Whether this represents a real difference in operating costs or a difference in accounting procedures is not clear from the reports.

Agent Middlemen

The third largest group of wholesalers consists of agent middlemen. (See Table 1, page 14.) They have been losing their share of the market, particularly since the end of World War II. An analysis of the changes in share by type of middleman reveals that the declines have been experienced by brokers, commission "merchants," and purchasing agents and resident buyers. Manufacturers and retailers, particularly, seem to be finding that they can dispense with the services of these agents and make the necessary market contacts themselves. The sales of purchasing agents and resident buyers actually declined nearly 30 percent between 1948 and 1963, the largest decline of any of the types of wholesalers reported in the *Census of Business.*

Selling agents have not shown any significant increase in share, and this situation would seem to indicate that manufacturers are assuming more marketing responsibility and are turning to manufacturers' agents or their own sales organizations, over which they have more control.

The greatest growth among agent middlemen has occurred in the sales of manufacturers' agents. Sales of these agents over the 1948–1963 period expanded 1½ times, and there was also a net increase of some 2,100 agent establishments. This growth reflects the entrance into the market of many small firms who prefer to sell through agents rather than attempt to operate their own sales organizations. It also reflects the very great importance of agents in the industrial field, an area which has depended heavily on highly specialized agents who know their market and can secure efficient coverage of it. Even fairly large manufacturers in the industrial field continue to use agents whenever they are able to secure and retain high-caliber people. Often, these companies will retain some agents after they have made a decision to sell directly to their customers.

The growing interest in foreign areas, both as markets and as sources of supply, probably accounts for the larger share which has gone to export and import agents. When firms first start to export or import they are more likely to use indirect channels, i.e., agents or other firms in this country, than to work directly with foreign middlemen.

The growth of large-scale food retailers, particularly voluntary chains, and the expansion of cooperative marketing activities for agricultural products could account for the declining share of commission merchants. In many cities, these middlemen have been plagued by crowded, inefficient working quarters, and their operating expenses have increased substantially.

Assemblers of Farm Products

Wholesalers engaged in the assembly of farm products decreased substantially in numbers in the postwar period (about 25 percent), and their sales declined 10 percent.[20] These changes reflect a general trend toward shortening the marketing channels for farm products as processors and large-scale retailers increase their direct buying from farmers.

Several changes have occurred which result in shorter channels for agricultural products. The increased specialization of poultry producers has led to more direct selling to processors, and these processors tend to be located closer to their source of supply. With the growth of milk shipments by bulk tank trucks, there has been a decline in country milk plants and cream stations. Meat slaughtering plants also have been located closer to livestock producers, and this likewise has increased direct buying. Cotton assemblers have become less important with the increase in direct-mill buying of cotton and the increased sales of cotton cooperatives.

In view of the major interest in steadily rising food prices, it is not likely that these trends will be reversed. Rather, it may be expected that continuing steps will be taken to reduce the costs of marketing farm products. Also, it is probable that some new types of integration will occur. One large milling company, for example, has recently entered the poultry business.

The Changing Retail Structure

While changes have been occurring in wholesaling, the retailing field has been equally dynamic. As already mentioned, the latter part of the nineteenth century and the early part of the twentieth were marked by

[20] *Census of Business, Wholesale Trade, United States Summary,* 1948 and 1963. Percentages calculated by author.

the development of the department store, mail-order house, and retail chain. If these institutions were a threat to merchant wholesalers, they also were a threat to the small, independent retailer. Consequently, predictions were sometimes made not only of the demise of the wholesaler but also of the elimination of a large percentage of the independent retail establishments, as well.

The first census of distribution, taken in 1929, reported approximately 1.4 million stores with average sales of about $33,000. Since 1939, the number of stores has stabilized at something over 1.7 million, but average sales have increased to $81,000, in constant dollars. Although large-scale retailers have been in the ascendancy since the period following the Civil War, most retailers are still comparatively small.

This follows from the need for retailers to be located close to their customers. Large-scale retailers—department stores, mail-order houses, and to a lesser extent chain units—tend to locate in large urban areas. In the neighborhood or suburban shopping center, the small town, and rural areas the small independent is the dominant institution. However, there will be some chain establishments in the latter areas, and an increasing number of retailers, especially in groceries, hardware, auto supplies, variety lines, and drugs, are becoming affiliated with voluntary chains or retailer-cooperative groups.

The general-mail-order houses, which might well have disappeared with the horse and buggy, drastically upgraded their lines and the quality of their catalogs, speeded up their order-filling routines, and by various devices made it increasingly easy and pleasant for the customer to buy. As a result, they have been able to hold their own. Over the period 1954–1963 sales of general-merchandise mail-order houses increased from $1.2 to $1.8 billion. In 1963, sales of mail-order establishments were about 1 percent of all retail sales. Sales were made from some 4,200 establishments, including the catalog offices of Sears and Ward.[21] It is clear that for the foreseeable future mail-order houses will continue to find favor in certain segments of the market. The largest general-merchandise house has, in fact, been conducting a national advertising campaign aimed at strengthening its image and broadening its market among the social classes.

The urban department store is another institution which has dis-

---

[21] U.S. Department of Commerce, Bureau of the Census, *Census of Business, Retail Trade, United States Summary,* 1963.

played considerable flexibility in the post-World War II period.[22] Faced with rising costs, traffic congestion in their downtown locations, a shift in population from the central city to the suburbs, and growing competition from discount stores, most department stores have acted aggressively. The most dramatic moves have been the establishment of suburban branches and, in some cases, the establishment of discount subsidiaries. Through buying-group affiliations they have been able to standardize quality, adopt private brands, and reduce buying costs, partly through large-scale group purchases. At the same time, they have capitalized on the promotional advantages, the service facilities, and the broad merchandise assortment which they have always had.

Over the period 1929–1963, the number of department stores and their share of market declined for a period and then increased. The increase in share has been particularly marked since 1958 and reflects the sales of department store branches which have been established in recent years.

During the past thirty years, two rather new retail institutions have become prominent, the supermarket and the discount house. Standardized definitions have not been developed for these establishments, and separate tabulations for them do not appear in the *Census of Business*.[23]

The Supermarket

The complex food store which has come to be known as the supermarket first appeared in the late twenties on the West Coast and then gained a foothold on the East Coast at the bottom of the depression of the thirties. With thousands of families suffering economic distress, the

---

[22] The Bureau of the Census defines department stores as establishments employing twenty-five people or more and selling furniture, home furnishings, appliances, household linens and dry goods, and apparel for the family. The definition contains a qualification regarding the balance of sales among these lines.

[23] A supermarket is a large, promotionally oriented, self-service store primarily engaged in the sale of a wide assortment of grocery products but handling other types of convenience goods as well.

A discount house is a general-merchandise store which operates at lower margins than conventional stores handling the same merchandise. It features price appeal and limited customer services. An increasing number of discount stores include a supermarket.

early "pine boards," [24] with their very low prices, drew families from many miles around—much farther than they would ordinarily travel to purchase groceries. The stores were poorly located in crude quarters. Their only service was to put merchandise on display, and their major and practically only appeal, at that time, was price.[25] These stores pioneered in self-service for groceries and featured a wide selection of food items which, in time, came to include fresh meat, produce, baked goods, and dairy products. Like their forerunner, the food chain, they did not offer credit or delivery services.

Though there was some question whether the supermarket was anything other than a depression phenomenon, and therefore likely to disappear with returning prosperity, it soon became evident that this institution filled a real need, and in a short space of time it carved a niche in the retail structure. Growth in a span of only thirty to thirty-five years has been rapid. A leading trade paper in the field, *Super Market Merchandising,* states that supermarkets accounted for 76.5 percent of grocery sales in 1964 and for nearly 40 percent of all retail sales.[26]

The modern supermarket has come a long way from the "pine board" of the Great Depression. Attractive and well lighted, conveniently located—frequently in a shopping center with ample parking space—this institution provides one-stop shopping for upwards of seven thousand grocery and nonfood items. This compares with less than a thousand items found in early supermarkets.[27]

The typical supermarket has 14,500 square feet (of which 70 percent

[24] The term "pine board" was used to describe some of the first supermarkets, which simply piled merchandise on wooden trestles in an abandoned warehouse or garage, put a price sign on it, and let customers help themselves.

[25] The opening-day advertisement of a Harrisburg, Pa., supermarket in 1933 carried the following items, among others: Maxwell House coffee, 24 cents per pound, private brand coffee, 15 cents per pound, oranges, 7 cents per dozen, bananas, 12 cents per dozen, butter, 19 cents per pound, eggs, 12 cents per dozen, Campbell's pork and beans, 3 cents, grapefruit, 2 cents each. "Food Fair Supermarkets," *Fortune* (June, 1950), pp. 99ff.

[26] "The True Look of the Super Market Industy 1964," *Super Market Merchandising* (May, 1965).

This source includes stores with sales in excess of $500,000 annually. This is about 15 percent of the total number of grocery stores. Nearly 72 percent of the supermarkets are operated by "chains" of four or more stores.

Another trade source, Super Market Institute, defines a supermarket as "a complete, departmentalized food store with a minimum sales volume of one million dollars a year and at least the grocery department fully self-service."

[27] *Grocery Business Annual Report, 1964, Progressive Grocer,* New York, 1964.

is selling space), an annual volume of nearly $1.5 million, and some 5,500 transactions per week. About 7 percent of the sales of new units is in nonfood items.[28]

The Discount House

For many years, some retail institutions have featured the sale of certain types of goods such as appliances, jewelry, and sporting goods at a discount. These were often "second-story" establishments. Some published catalogs, some sold only to cardholders, but they all featured limited services and "wholesale" prices.[29]

Since World War II, this institution has burgeoned rapidly and is now found in virtually all large cities and along heavily traveled highways. Trade sources report nearly three thousand discount stores (with areas in excess of 10,000 square feet) in 1964.[30] During the five-year period 1960–1964, sales of this class of large discount houses rose from $2 billion to $10.8 billion, an increase of nearly 450 percent at a time when retail sales overall were increasing 19 percent, and department store sales were increasing 15 percent.

Like the supermarket, discount stores have clearly found a niche in the retail field. Also, like their aggressive retail predecessors—chain stores, mail-order houses, and department stores—they were opposed by competing retail institutions (including the above) and by some manufacturers. But, as occurred with respect to supermarkets, the competition "joined them." In recent years, several department store and chain-store organizations have established discount subsidiaries, and some of

---

28 *Ibid.*

29 References to pre-World War II discounting operations may be found in Stanley C. Hollander, "The Discount House," *Journal of Marketing* (July, 1953).

See also F. W. Gilchrist, "The Discount House," *Journal of Marketing* (January, 1953).

Gilchrist identified nine types of discounters: (1) Dealers who operate entirely on a discount basis with admission by card; (2) dealers who stress discount sales but whose primary emphasis is on ordinary trade; (3) dealers who conduct an informal discount business by referrals or catering to occupational groups; (4) the discount broker ("He can get it for you 'at cost plus ten' and rarely stocks merchandise."); (5) the employees' association; (6) employer's purchasing services; (7) repairmen who can buy at "cost plus ten"; (8) building contractors; (9) others, including department store contract departments.

30 "The True Look of the Discount Industry 1964," *Discount Merchandiser*, New York, 1965.

these compete directly with the established stores of the parent organization.

Trade estimates indicate that total sales of discount stores are about 75 percent of department store sales.[31] Annual volume per store was approximately \$3.5 million in 1964. This is more than double the average discount-store volume only five years earlier.

One of the most significant retail developments of recent years has been the expansion of discount stores into the supermarket business. Sales of supermarkets associated with discount stores have increased from \$400 million in 1960 to \$2.8 billion in 1964. The latter figure represents about one-quarter of all discount-store volume. Nearly 40 percent of the discount stores larger than 10,000 square feet had supermarket operations in 1964.

In addition to food departments in discount stores, separate discount supermarkets are also operating. These are characterized by lower prices than regular supermarkets, fewer items, no trading stamps, reduced customer services, and cheaper construction.[32]

The Wheel of Retailing

Some years ago, Prof. Malcolm McNair presented his *wheel-of-retailing* concept to explain the evolution of the retail structure.[33] He hypothesized that new forms of retailing enter the market at the "low-status" end. The new institution features low prices and low margins as a result of reduced services, less-convenient locations, and a reduction in promotion. The chain store—notably in the grocery and variety fields—the mail-order house, the supermarket, and the discount store are examples of retail institutions which began with a low-margin, low-price appeal.

As time goes on, there is a tendency for these establishments to trade up. They increase their services and, frequently, the range and quality of their goods as well. They appeal more to middle- and upper-income

[31] *Ibid.*

[32] *The Super Market Industry Speaks, 1964,* Super Market Institute, Chicago, 1964, p. 19.

[33] Malcolm P. McNair, "Significant Trends and Developments in the Postwar Period," in A. B. Smith (ed.), *Competitive Distribution in a Free High-level Economy and Its Implications for the University,* The University of Pittsburgh Press, Pittsburgh, Pa., 1957, p. 17.

groups and tend to lose their price appeal to low-income groups. As their status rises, their vulnerability to the next form of innovation increases. Growing respectability seems to be accompanied by rising costs. This has occurred in the supermarket field and is now under way with regard to discount houses.

Supermarket margins increased from about 16 percent in 1950 to approximately 20 percent fifteen years later. The steady upward movement of supermarket costs and gross margins during recent years is indicated in Table 6.

TABLE 6

Typical Supermarket Operating Results (Percent of Sales)

	1963	1962	1961	1960	1959	1958	1957	1954
Gross profit	19.75	19.46	18.83	18.64	18.26	18.12	18.11	17.37
Total expenses	17.94	17.71	17.44	17.12	16.27	16.19	16.04	14.72

Source: *The Super Market Industry Speaks, 1964,* Super Market Institute, Chicago, 1964.

Likewise, the discount store in some areas has improved its image. Establishments are found in better locations, and the store may have the appearance of a department store branch. The changing character of the discount store is reflected in the following description of Polk Bros., Chicago, one of the best-known discount operations in the country.

> Polk Bros. maintains a well-developed business philosophy which includes the following principles: (1) only brand-name merchandise; (2) wide selection of models and makes; (3) convenient locations with parking facilities; (5) open 84 hours a week, including Sundays; (5) adequate force of well-informed, customer-oriented sales personnel; (6) next-day delivery of purchases; (7) credit availability; (8) low prices (an average margin of 18%); (9) repair service and adjustment service; and (10) trade-in privileges. One might call the operation a "full-service discount house." [34]

Not all retail institutions have followed the "wheel" pattern. The department store began as a high-quality, multiline store which offered many services. Some department stores later applied the wheel-of-retailing concept to their own operations by opening "budget-priced"

[34] John S. Wright, "Leaders in Marketing—Sol Polk," *Journal of Marketing* (April, 1966), pp. 61–62.

basement stores. Hollander uncovered other retailing developments which did not support the concept.[35] These were (1) the introduction of supermarkets in underdeveloped countries largely at the top of the social and price scales; (2) vigorous price competition among Japanese department stores during the first three decades of this century; (3) the record of price cutting by traditional, well-established British merchants in the 1880s and 1890s; (4) the introduction of automatic merchandising as a high-cost, high-margin, high-convenience type of retailing in the United States; and (5) the establishment in the United States of department store branches and planned shopping centers as exclusive-type institutions in prestige locations.

Some of Hollander's examples are drawn from other countries, and it is not clear that the concept applies to other economies, since their retail needs and their histories differ from ours. A supermarket in an underdeveloped country, for example, is likely to be far better than anything else there. Furthermore, such transplanted institutions are likely to appear at about the same level at which they exist in the "exporting" country. Supermarkets, for example, took root in Europe in the post-World War II period, not in the 1930s.

Some department stores in the United States, as well as other types of retailers, such as variety chains, have established discount-house subsidiaries. At the same time, however, they have expanded their regular operations into suburban branch stores. But the latter are not new institutions, they are simply offshoots of the parent organization and reach about the same class markets.

Vending machine operations are a high-margin activity because they offer a major service, convenience. Products are sold in small quantities, and there may be additional packaging costs. Some of the machines, especially those handling food, are complicated affairs which involve a substantial investment.

It is apparent that the wheel-of-retailing concept will not explain every innovation in the retail structure. However, it seems equally true that the American public will patronize a retail institution which offers goods of an acceptable quality at a low price even though it eliminates some of the services offered by competing stores. The shape of the successor to the supermarket and the discount store is not yet evident, but

[35] Stanley C. Hollander, "The Wheel of Retailing," *Journal of Marketing* (July, 1960), p. 40.

one can confidently expect that such an institution will appear at the appropriate time.

Countervailing Power

Under the classical conception of the competitive model, where there are many sellers handling essentially the same product, no one seller is able to exercise economic power in pricing because of the presence of competitors. As an increasing number of industries have moved in the direction of oligopoly, however, the old competitive restraints on prices frequently have become inoperative. Short of some form of governmental intervention, this appears to leave buyers pretty much at the mercy of the oligopolists.

The solution to this problem came in the form of large-scale buyers, primarily retailers, who could meet the oligopolist on his own ground. The growing concentration of power in industry brought about a similar concentration in power among retailers in order to offset the decline in price competition among sellers. Economists refer to this phenomenon as *countervailing power* ". . . the existence of market power creates an incentive to the organization of another position of power that neutralizes it." [36]

Countervailing power has developed in retailing primarily because price is so very important in most trades; and the most direct way to influence price from the buying side is to build a buying-power bloc which is strong enough to put pressure on oligopolists. Such retail blocs exist in the form of centrally owned chains, cooperative chains, consumer cooperatives, mail-order houses, and department stores—both individually and as buying groups. These retailers exercise power in various ways, in addition to demanding the most favorable prices and terms. They can ask for local advertising support, special shipping arrangements, and special merchandise-return privileges. They can concentrate their orders with one or a few suppliers and can exert pressure even by the threat of withdrawing purchases. Furthermore, they can encourage new sources of supply and develop their own brands.

There is a close tie between the wheel-of-retailing concept and the countervailing-power concept, as applied to retailing. Both hinge on the

[36] John K. Galbraith, *American Capitalism,* rev. ed., Houghton Mifflin Company, Boston, 1956, p. 111.

importance of price in retailing. Both the innovations basic to the wheel concept and the incentive that leads to bigness in retailing derive from the need to attract consumers of convenience and shopping goods, particularly, through the use of the price appeal. Furthermore, these factors make it virtually certain that large-scale retailers of various types will continue to be of great importance in the marketing structure.

The Merchandise-Service Mix

Retailers offer a mix of merchandise and services, and several resultant combinations are possible: high product quality–low service cost; high product quality–high service cost; low product quality–low service cost; etc. Usually, retailers match a given merchandise policy with a particular service policy and, consequently, the consumer has little choice concerning the combination of goods and services he will receive.[37]

Retailers generally have believed that the market segment toward which they direct their efforts prefers a particular quality level of merchandise; once this quality level of merchandise is established, it is usually paralleled by the level of services. Thus a store which carries top-quality lines tends to give maximum services as well; and the store which caters to lower-income groups will reduce the services offered accordingly. The whole range of store operation (merchandise and services) is, therefore, at one level. The customer who patronizes the high-quality store, for example, pays for the services provided whether he wants them or not.

In most department stores, more than one socioeconomic group is reached, and the quality of merchandise among the departments is varied to meet the needs of these groups. However, except for variations in physical facilities by department, the services offered are basically the same. The customer, therefore, does not have full choice in the range of merchandise quality *and* the level of services he desires.

In order to permit customers to secure the *services* they want in addition to the *goods* they want, Regan indicates that retailers need to move toward the stage at which customers can select their own combination

---

[37] William J. Regan, "The Stages of Retail Development," in Reavis Cox, Wroe Alderson, and Stanley Shapiro (eds.), *Theory in Marketing: Second Series,* Richard D. Irwin, Inc., Homewood, Ill., 1964, pp. 139ff.

of goods and services rather than having to accept the limited combinations now provided. This would restrict the number of store contacts a customer would have to make and would reduce the time and effort spent in shopping.

> One can foresee multichannel systems of retail service in a single store and customers choosing freely, item by item, the particular combination of merchandise and service which is desired. No single store today is organized to offer all combinations of goods and services to its customers. . . . The largest hurdle is to associate effectively the seesaw combination of relatively high-cost merchandise with average- and low-cost retail services and relatively low-cost merchandise with average- and high-cost retail services.[38]

Such large-scale retailers as mail-order houses, department stores, supermarkets, and discount stores have broadened their merchandise assortments. In some cases, for example mail-order houses, they have broadened their services as well. Supermarkets and discount houses have tended to restrict their services. Regan would say that these retailers have moved into "multiplex" trading but they have not reached the ultimate flexibility of "omniplex" trading.

Retailers will need to find ways of meeting the desires of limited-income families who want high-quality goods at a low markup (and, therefore, a low level of service). Conversely, there is a status-conscious market in which the level of service is all-important, perhaps more important than the goods; and there are many gradations in between.

Limitations to Innovation by Wholesalers and Retailers

The preceding sections have outlined the major evolutionary developments in wholesale and retail trade in the United States. Compared with the pattern in other countries (as will be noted in the next chapter), these developments have occurred in a comparatively short period of time. Nevertheless, middlemen, typically, have been reluctant to change their methods of doing business. Rather than taking the lead in improving their operations or in meeting the changing needs of their customers, established tradesmen have commonly been satisfied with the *status quo.*

Many of the changes at the wholesale level resulted from pressures

---

[38] *Ibid.*

brought to bear by manufacturers and large retail organizations; and most of the retail innovations, at least of an institutional type, come from new entrants into retailing. The early growth of supermarkets in the 1930s and the establishment of large general-merchandise discount houses in the post-World War II period resulted from the efforts of aggressive pioneers who entered the market with a bold new idea. Likewise, the first chains and department stores, some voluntary chains, and the two large general-mail-order houses were established by people who saw an opportunity for a new kind of enterprise.

Several factors account for the sluggishness of established wholesalers and retailers and this tendency to stick to tried operating patterns. One has to do with management goals.

> . . . small retailers tend to have relatively static expectations. That is they are interested in reaching and maintaining a given scale of operation, and reject opportunities for growth beyond this point. Such retailers tend to view their demand curve as being relatively fixed. Thus, they are inclined to resist innovation because it presumably cannot improve their position and could conceivably disrupt a reasonably attractive *status quo*.[39]

Another factor which applies to both wholesalers and retailers in several product lines is the tendency to work and take action as a group, generally through an industry trade association. Groups are seldom innovative, so again any action taken is likely to be in defense of their present position. Group action makes itself most evident in lobbying activities in connection with proposed legislation affecting the industry. The prime interest of such groups is usually to "protect" their industry against all comers, including Federal and state governments.

When changes are finally made by the established channel units, they are typically only enough to meet the competitive threat. They are essentially defensive rather than offensive in nature, and the speed and extent of the change will vary with the severity of the threat. The initiative has been taken by another institution in the channel, and the steps taken by the industry as a whole are intended simply to protect a niche. The initiative remains with the pioneering firms; they continue to be the aggressors, and their smaller competitors tend to fight a rear-

[39] Bert C. McCammon, Jr., "Alternative Explanations of Institutional Change and Channel Evolution," in *Toward Scientific Marketing,* American Marketing Association, Chicago, 1964. This paper is a particularly good exposition of the factors underlying changes in channel institutions.

guard action against them. The reaction is likely to be measured and deliberate unless the new developments strike at the foundation of the firm. Then, more drastic action must be taken and taken quickly, and we may see the rapid spread of certain developments throughout the industry.

This explains the rapid growth of voluntary chains in such lines as groceries and hardware, in some areas, since World War II. Independent, unaffiliated retailers were literally threatened with extinction in some markets. Consequently, over the span of a very few years virtually all retailers had to find some way of affiliating with an organized group in order to survive. When this has occurred, a new state of equilibrium is attained.

Political Action and Channel Innovation

The struggles between channel innovators and existing middlemen, particularly wholesalers and the smaller retailers, have often led to political action by those who are threatened by competitive change. In the Depression of the 1930s, these economic and political forces resulted in legislation at the Federal and state levels which was intended to ease the competitive pressures on small retailers particularly. The Robinson-Patman Act (competitive marketing practices), and the Miller-Tydings Act (resale-price maintenance—often called "fair trade") were passed at the Federal level. State legislation included supporting price maintenance laws, unfair-practices (minimum markup) laws, and "antichain" taxes.

As events turned out, the innovators succeeded in spite of legislative obstacles. With respect to the Robinson-Patman Act, Palamountain observes:

> Even had the original bill passed unamended, it is doubtful whether mass distribution could really have been crippled by such a shallow and patchworklike attempt to hobble the competitive vigor of mass distributors through an attack on some of the surface reflections of the revolution which had already taken place in the channels of trade. It was an attempt to strike at the symptoms of change not at its causes . . . in this sector, the economy was too dynamic to be channeled to an important degree by the amount of governmental regulation which could be evoked by the political strength mustered by independents.[40]

[40] Joseph C. J. Palamountain, *The Politics of Distribution,* Harvard University Press, Cambridge, Mass., 1955, p. 233.

The fair-trade laws, state and Federal, had been aggressively supported by organized business groups, notably the retail druggists. With respect to these efforts Palamountain concluded:

> Thus even a hasty glance at contemporary conditions in the trade indicates how limited were the economic fruits gained by the organized druggists. The consumer lost a political battle, but the druggists did not gain as much as they expected. They were unable to shackle to any important degree the basic competitive dynamism of the economy.[41]

The structural changes which have occurred make it reasonably clear that intertype competition has been a significant factor in reducing marketing costs and improving the technology of distribution. As a result, consumers have been given some relief from price exploitation by established retailers.

---

[41] *Ibid.*, p. 253. Palamountain analyzes the relative political power exercised by retail grocers and druggists. He concludes that retail grocery associations have not been very effective politically. There seems to be a lack of cohesion among grocers which probably results from the fact that they constitute a very mixed group in terms of background, retailing experience, and financial position. Druggists have been more successful politically. By virtue of their professional training, they are a more homogeneous group and also benefit from the entry standards set by the states.

3

Marketing Channels in Other Countries

Each country has a marketing structure which is to some degree unique. As countries move toward a higher degree of industrialization, however, they tend to adopt the marketing institutions of their more highly developed neighbors, although frequently not to the same degree nor in quite the same form. If one were to place the countries of the world along a continuum, with the United States at one extreme and the new nations of Africa at the other, it would be apparent that there are discernible patterns of development.

As countries become more highly industrialized and their standard of living rises, certain changes in marketing structures and institutions appear. For example, the small, limited-line retail establishment gradually is displaced by large-scale retailers such as chain stores, supermarkets, and department stores. This displacement does not continue unchecked and does not extend to all lines of goods. It occurs particularly in food, other types of convenience goods, and soft goods. In the same lines, there is also a shift toward self-service. This tendency was clearly shown in one study which compared the per capita production indexes of some twenty countries with the percentage of self-service stores.[1] At the top of the list in both categories were the United States, United Kingdom, Switzerland, Canada, Sweden, and Denmark. At the lower end were India, Mexico, Spain, Venezuela, and Italy. The latter group of coun-

[1] Edward W. Cundiff, "Concepts in Comparative Retailing," *Journal of Marketing* (January, 1965), pp. 59–63.

tries, of course, is not at the bottom of the industrial scale. Data for the really underdeveloped areas were not available, but self-service activity in this group is virtually nonexistent.

Retailers in the convenience-goods and soft-goods fields frequently join cooperative organizations which give them some of the operating advantages of their chain competitors; and at the same time that some independent retailers are dropping out, others are appearing in durables and specialty lines.

The changes in retailing in France are typical of the evolving retail structures of many countries. During the past fifteen years, the share of sales obtained by large-scale retailers has about doubled. The number of variety chain stores increased from 150 to over 600. At the beginning of 1965 there were 450 supermarkets, while between 1954 and 1964 the number of independent grocers decreased 20 percent.[2]

In the United States since the end of World War II, there has been a marked growth in suburban shopping centers, which are usually dominated by large-scale retailers. Thus far, this aspect of retail change has not occurred to any appreciable degree in foreign countries. Differences in shopping behavior probably account for this. United States suburban shoppers are dependent on automobiles. In other countries, city dwellers shop on foot in neighborhood areas.

Perhaps because the United States has assumed the position of industrial leader, it has experienced a development in marketing methods which places it in the vanguard with respect to marketing activities. Some countries have attained a preeminence in certain industrial spheres, but similar examples in marketing are hard to discover. Consequently, many of the changes in marketing-channel structures around the world have been similar to, and sometimes patterned after, changes that have occurred here. The changes are not necessarily identical with ours, but the similarities are apparent.

One area which has had an evolution in marketing structure that parallels ours is Australia. The emulation of American institutions has taken an unexpected form in this country, however:

> One somewhat singular aspect of Australian retailing lends support to the thesis that American marketing methods will work effectively in Australia. At times, the transplanted American might be forgiven for wonder-

[2] Michel David, "Developments in the Structure of Distribution in France: A Moderate Degree of Concentration," *Journal of Retailing* (Summer, 1965), pp. 34 ff.

ing if he had really left home. Woolworth and Penney stores stand close by on the main street of Brisbane. In Sydney, shoppers may patronize Macy's where "It's smart to be thrifty." There are many opportunities in other parts of Australia for housewives to buy groceries at Big Bear, Food Fair, Safeway, and Stop-and-Shop.

Yet none of these retailers has any connection or ever has had with firms of the same name in the United States. However much Americans might wonder about the choice of names or speculate on the number of Sydney-siders to whom Macy's is familiar or of Brisbaneites who have heard of the American Penney's, Australian retailers are convinced that such names are effective.[3]

Australian wholesaling, likewise, has faced much the same pressures as in the United States. Manufacturers increasingly sell direct, either with or without wholesale branches. On the other side, retail chains, particularly in the food field, operate their own wholesale organizations.

The countries whose channel structures are most similar to those of the United States (other than Canada) are the industrial leaders of Western Europe, particularly Great Britain and Western Germany.

British Marketing Structure

The ratio of retail stores to population is about the same in Britain as in the United States; and in both countries the dominant retail institution has been the small independent store. There are differences in the retail structure, however. One of the most significant is that cooperatives handle about 10 percent of British retail sales.

Cooperatives have been of major importance in Britain since the flannel weavers of Rochdale established the Rochdale Society of Equitable Pioneers in 1844 in response to a desire to improve retail practices.[4] Their share of retail sales has declined somewhat in recent years, however, as a result of the growth of "multiples" (organizations other than department stores and cooperatives with ten or more establishments)

[3] John S. Ewing, "Marketing in Australia," *Journal of Marketing* (April, 1962), pp. 54–58.
[4] The operating principles of the Rochdale Society became the model for consumer cooperatives in many countries. The Rochdale plan provided for open membership without restrictions, one vote per member regardless of the number of shares held, sales at going market prices coupled with patronage dividends, a limited return on invested capital, all sales for cash, and the use of educational activities to stimulate cooperative spirit and loyalty.

and supermarkets. Their left-wing affiliation, management limitations, and declining dividends, coupled with the greater attraction of competitive food outlets, have weakened the position of cooperatives; and there is some doubt whether they can continue to hold their own.[5] Over the period 1950 to 1961, the retail share of the multiples increased from 22.6 to 27.6 percent while the share of cooperatives dropped slightly, from 11.2 to 10.8 percent.[6] The development of chains has, likewise, been one factor in the very limited consumer interest in cooperatives in the United States.

Another factor in the British food trade has been the growth of "mobile shops." These are specially designed vehicles (some of a battery-electric type) which provide inside service, fluorescent lighting, washing facilities, and cold-storage containers. They are operated by driver-salesmen and travel a regularly scheduled route. They tend to specialize in one segment of the food field; the largest number are in dry groceries, meat, and produce. Compared with established stores, productivity (average sales per person) may be as much as 75 percent higher. Many of the vehicles are operated by cooperative societies. Mobile shops account for some 3 percent of retail food sales and serve particularly rural areas and new housing developments where stores have been slow in appearing. Some units are also found in nonfood areas, particularly dry goods, apparel, and hairdressing.[7]

British department stores, like their counterparts in many countries (excluding the United States), have full-fledged food departments. Otherwise, they match United States department stores with respect to merchandise lines and breadth of services. Several department stores operate real estate offices and insurance departments.[8]

In recent years, the share of sales of British department stores has declined. This follows a pattern which existed in the United States for many years but which has recently been reversed as the result of new department store branches in suburban shopping centers—a development which has not occurred to the same extent in Britain.

Postwar Britain has experienced a rapidly growing mail-order busi-

[5] Harper W. Boyd and Ivan Piercy, "Retailing in Great Britain," *Journal of Marketing* (January, 1963), pp. 29–35.
[6] *Ibid.*
[7] "Retailing on the Move," *The Economist* (Mar. 14, 1959), pp. 991–992.
[8] M. B. Tracey, "British Retail Institutions," *Journal of Retailing* (Summer, 1957), pp. 93ff.

ness. Some of the most successful firms use agency operations. Agents are women, "who handle between five and fifteen customers, and who take round the catalogue, collect orders, deliver goods, and collect weekly payments." [9] Commissions range from 10 to 12½ percent, and customers receive credit up to thirty-eight weeks. Catalog costs run from 30 shillings to £2 each.

Other mail-order houses send catalogs through the mail, as American firms do; but one group, the "Saturday Squares," reach their markets by advertising on weekends in the newspapers. The latter houses handle a limited line of goods. Unlike United States mail-order firms, British companies do not sell on a price basis. In fact, prices may be slightly higher than in retail stores. Instead, their main appeal is liberal credit. Some retail stores also sell on a mail-order basis. Harrods, for example, does a worldwide mail-order business.[10]

In addition to growing mail-order sales, Britain, along with other leading markets, has experienced a postwar influx of American direct-selling companies.[11] Cosmetics firms have been among the first to enter; but firms selling household products, costume jewelry, and reference books have been close behind. Even home-party-plan sales techniques, which have been successful in the United States, are being introduced overseas. Some companies ship from the United States; others license local producers or lease production facilities. A small but growing number of American direct-sales firms operate their own overseas factories.

Retailing in Western Europe

The small, independent retailer is the dominant retail institution throughout Western Europe; and many of them are small indeed in comparison with American stores. These establishments not only are small in size but carry restricted lines of goods. This fragmentation is still a major characteristic of European retailing, and consumer buying habits are geared to it to such a degree that changes in buying patterns are likely to occur quite slowly. The American housewife expects to buy

[9] "Who's for Mail Order?" *The Economist* (Mar. 27, 1965), pp. 1406–1407.
[10] *Ibid.*
[11] "The Overseas Boom in Door-to-door Selling," *Dun's Review and Modern Industry* (November, 1964), pp. 35ff.

virtually all food items in a single store, and the same is true for drugs and toilet goods, hardware, and household products. The foreign housewife, however, even in advanced countries, generally visits several stores to meet her needs in these lines.

> A Finnish consumer must visit four stores in order to purchase the array of merchandise that the typical American drug store carries. These are the apothecary, dispensing prescriptions and over-the-counter drugs; the "chemical" shop which stocks toilet goods; the "paper" shop which stocks stationery supplies; and the "kiosk" which carries candy and soft drinks [12]
>
> . . . . .
>
> . . . the American supermarket equals the French *epicerie* (groceries), plus *crémerie* (dairy products, eggs), plus *charcuterie* (specialty meats), plus *boulangerie* (bread), plus *patisserie* (pastries), plus *droguerie* (household cleaning supplies), plus *poissonnerie* (fish), plus *boucherie* (fresh meat), etc. [13]

Similarly, the Spanish housewife faces about the same array of food establishments, unless she is patronizing one of the large city markets. However, she is basically dependent on neighborhood stores.

Although food sales are still handled primarily by small, independent retailers, consumer cooperatives in some countries—for example, France and Germany—have been growing. Cooperatives have been of particular significance in northern Europe. About one-third of Finnish retail trade is handled by cooperatives. More important, however, has been the growth of retailer-cooperative chains.

The first European voluntary chain, the "Spar" organization, was established in the Netherlands in 1932. There were also prewar voluntary chain activities of a limited nature in Germany and Sweden. It was not until the early 1950s, however, that voluntary-chain development really got underway. The first growth occurred in the Netherlands (where 70 percent of the independent grocers belong to voluntary groups) and Germany and then spread to France, Belgium, Switzerland, Austria, and the Scandinavian countries. Among the northern European countries, Great Britain was the last to experience voluntary-chain development. During the last decade, several European voluntary-chain organizations have extended their activities beyond the countries

[12] A. J. Alton, "Marketing in Finland," *Journal of Marketing* (July, 1963), pp. 47–51.

[13] S. Watson Dunn, "French Retailing and the Common Market," *Journal of Marketing* (January, 1962), pp. 19–22.

in which they were originally established and now operate throughout Western Europe. International Spar has 225 wholesale and 30,000 retail members.

European voluntary-chain activity is primarily in the grocery field, but one organization in hardware and another in apparel were established in France.[14] One observer of the French marketing system indicates that many retailers are too small or too "individualistic" to join cooperative groups.[15]

Many of Germany's soft-goods retailers have set up their own cooperative buying groups, and nearly twenty such groups operate central buying facilities for some seven thousand shops.[16]

Centrally owned chains have become important in some countries, particularly in the food field. Germany has some ninety food chains which handle about 10 percent of the retail grocery business. France has about the same number.

The fastest growth of chains has occurred in the variety field. Variety chain stores in France increased from 150 in 1950 to 600 in 1965.[17] In Italy, the only sizable chain-store organizations are Upim and Standa, each having about one hundred variety-type stores.[18]

About 90 percent of Germany's department store volume is handled by chains.[19] Four chains, each of which operates about fifty stores, dominate the field. In Italy, department stores have a high-price image and, consequently, there are few of any type, and only nine in the country.[20]

Large-scale Retail Innovations

The most recent large-scale retail innovations in the United States have been the supermarket and the discount house; and both these institutions have gained a foothold in Europe in the postwar period. The

---

[14] Organization for Economic Cooperation and Development (OECD), *Voluntary Chains in Europe: Structure, Organization, Results,* Paris, 1961 (mimeographed).

[15] David, *op cit.*

[16] Louis de Salaberry, "How Suppliers Can Reach Germany's Big Purchasers," *International Commerce* (Nov. 26, 1962), pp. 10–11.

[17] David, *op. cit.*

[18] Paul E. Allvin, "Retail Distribution Channels Inadequate for Burgeoning Industrial Economy," *International Commerce* (Jan. 27, 1964), pp. 16–17.

[19] "Germany's Retail Trade Agitated by Inroads of Discount Houses," *International Commerce* (Nov. 26, 1962), pp. 15–16.

[20] Allvin, *op. cit.*

supermarket has experienced a very rapid growth, particularly during the last ten years. In France, for example, the first supermarket was established in 1957, and there were 450 by the beginning of 1965.[21]

European supermarkets are smaller than those in the United States, carry a more limited line of goods, and do not provide comparable parking facilities. Under the definition adopted by the International Self-Service Institute of Cologne, a supermarket should have at least 400 square meters (4,300 square feet) of selling space. American supermarkets tend to be two or three times this size.[22]

One significant aspect of supermarket development in Europe is that the initiative has come from organizations outside the grocery trade:

> Initiative has come in Britain mainly from . . . a Candian biscuit and bread manufacturer, a large milk chain, and a department-store group. In Italy, three-quarters of the new supermarkets have been set up by retail chains like Rinascente-Upim and Standa which were already experienced in the organization of mass distribution but not previously very active in the food trade. The biggest supermarkets firm in France is controlled by the Brussels department store l'Innovation. In Spain, the first 50 supermarkets were set up by the government.[23]

This situation presents an interesting parallel to the development of supermarkets in the United States. The first supermarkets here were opened by new entrepreneurs rather than by the established food chains. It was some years after the supermarket appeared before the food chains began to open establishments of this type. The supermarket was considered a depression phenomenon, and the food chains decided to "wait and see." However, since supermarkets had become well entrenched here by the end of World War II, it is curious that the idea was not taken up by European chains operating in the food trade. In some countries, such as Italy and Spain, strong food chains had not been established, and in these countries outside entrepreneurs were necessary.

The "discount house" is the newest type of retail institution in Europe; but, like other adaptations, these establishments are not modeled exactly on the United States store of the same name. Whereas the

---

[21] David, *op. cit.*

[22] Members of the Super Market Institute (U.S.) indicated in 1965 that the "ideal" supermarket should have 13,400 square feet of selling space.

[23] John C. Abbott, "Food Marketing in Western Europe Today," *Journal of Marketing* (April, 1963), pp. 17–22.

United States discount house began in appliances, jewelry, and other durables, the European establishment has tended to emphasize food and soft-goods lines. More recently, durable goods have been added. The American heritage of these establishments is recognized, however. In Germany, for example, the English word "discount" is in general use.

Not all the innovations in food retailing have originated in the United States. In Stockholm, there is the Hemkop (Home Shop), which sells food products and a limited range of nonfoods at a discount, using a catalog, telephone orders, and home-delivery service. The entrepreneur felt that in a country where few families shop by car, a low-priced, home-delivery operation would be more profitable than a self-service supermarket. Operating costs are reported to be 12.5 percent versus 13.8 percent for a self-service store there.[24]

Impact of the European Common Market

The long-term evolution of the European Common Market will have a substantial impact on the European distribution system. The markets of wholesalers and retailers will no longer be limited by national boundaries. This will enable the more aggressive wholesalers and large-scale retailers to expand their geographical markets. Already, this has occurred among some of the larger voluntary chains in the food field. Spar International is in eleven countries, ranging from Spain to Sweden and from Italy to Great Britain. Vivo International, Centra, and VéGé are also in several Western European countries. All these groups have their headquarters in the Netherlands.[25]

As time goes on, it may be expected that a similar expansion will be undertaken by chain stores and department stores. There will also be opportunities for a growing mail-order business, on the part of both specialized mail-order houses and other large retailers, especially department stores.

As these developments are paralleled by a rising standard of living, there will be a much-needed upgrading in retail wholesale operations. At the retail level, this will take the form of larger and better assortments of stocks, improved store facilities, and more promotion. Re-

---

24 "A Supermarket without a Store," *Business Week* (Jan. 11, 1964), pp. 100–102.
25 OECD, *op. cit.*

tail fragmentation, especially in convenience and shopping goods, will gradually disappear. It may be expected, however, that new types of specialty stores will arise, and many of them will be relatively small.

The position of the merchant wholesaler may well be strengthened, since he will offer manufacturers the opportunity to reach wide markets efficiently. This will require that wholesalers reexamine both their lines and their services in order to meet the needs of manufacturers and retailers. The position of the specialty wholesaler in both consumer and industrial goods should be enhanced. The Common Market should also offer rewards to industrial distributors geared to serve particular market segments.

The end result could be a multinational regional distribution pattern involving middlemen equipped to serve this type of market. Undoubtedly, many of the existing middlemen will be quick to seize these opportunities. However, in the light of past experience, it is probable that this development will await new entrants. It is also likely, and in fact probable, that some of these entrants will be American firms and entrepreneurs from other European countries.

Marketing behind the Iron Curtain

The State has taken over most marketing activities in the iron-curtain countries. In the Soviet Union, there are two main trade networks:

> The government store network is the largest and is located exclusively in urban areas. The cooperative store network consists primarily of rural outlets with some city branches. Both networks have their own wholesale and supply systems. A third minor type of outlet located in both rural and urban areas is the *kolkhoz* (collective farm) market. The latter has no formal wholesale or supply system and is administered through the government store administrative hierarchy.[26]

Most government stores, including such establishments as farmers' markets, mail-order establishments, public eating facilities, sidewalk stalls and stands, and even vending machine installations are supervised by the ministries of trade. Drugstores, however, are under the Ministry of Health, newsstands are the responsibility of the Ministry of Communication, and the Ministry of Culture operates a network of bookstores.[27]

[26] Marshall I. Goldman, *Soviet Marketing: Distribution in a Controlled Economy,* The Free Press of Glencoe, New York, 1963, p. 11.
[27] *Ibid.,* p. 16.

Managers of government retail stores are under the control of the local trade organization, or *torg*. In large cities there may be several *torgi* for different kinds of goods, and they may operate some wholesale facilities. Above the *torgi* are the republic ministries of trade, which administer both retail trade and a substantial share of wholesale trade. At times, final control over distribution has rested in a centralized, overriding ministry, but in recent years the tendency has been to decentralize control and to employ it at the republic level.

Stores in rural areas are operated by "consumer cooperatives." However, these are not cooperatives of the Western, or Rochdale, type. Rural residents are organized into village cooperatives (*sel'po*), regional cooperatives (*raipo*), or farm cooperatives (*sovkhoz-rabkoopy*); but these cooperatives are not democratically operated autonomous units. Prices are set by the ministry of trade, and decisions concerning operating directors, member dues, and merchandise stocks are made not at the local level but further up in the cooperative and governmental hierarchy.[28]

The degree of government control over the distribution of consumer goods varies. Consumer goods of major importance such as flour, sugar, leather, and cotton and wool fabric are centrally allocated. The control over items of lower priority is decentralized and may rest with the *torgi*. The *torgi* may place some orders directly with the factory. In other cases, orders move through regional warehouses (wholesalers) back to the original shipping warehouse near the point of production.

Orders for locally produced goods may be placed by the retail stores directly with the producer. Actually, the assumption that the planning agencies within the Soviet government direct the flow of every piece of merchandise is not correct. Store managers, at least of larger stores, may have some leeway concerning the goods stocked and may reject poor-quality merchandise. Goods that do not sell may be transferred to stores in other localities or moved through local, horizontal-type trade fairs at which surplus goods are displayed.[29]

Wholesalers place orders with suppliers at the beginning of the year, working from samples prepared by manufacturers and frequently displayed in industry trade fairs. It is estimated that the trade ministries

[28] *Ibid.,* pp. 34–35.
[29] D. Maynard Phelps, "Soviet Marketing—Stronger than We Think," *Harvard Business Review* (July, 1961), pp. 69–80.

now handle 60 percent of the wholesale trade in consumer goods.[30]

Wholesale units are of two types. One category is the shipping warehouse, at the point of production. The other is the receiving warehouse, which makes delivery to retail organizations.[31] Some wholesale units operate processing and manufacturing facilities, particularly for food products. As another example, the jewelry trade organization has facilities for the manufacture of jewelry.[32]

The distribution of consumer goods is based partly on industry production plans and partly on the orders originating from retailers.

> The provision of goods is brought about by measures taken at the top and bottom of the chain of command. It is a circular procedure. On the one hand, allocation plans are made at upper echelons and handed down through channels. On the other hand, specific requests and orders of stores and trade organizations are sent upward asking for a quota of goods or seeking shipment of an already authorized quota. In turn, the higher authorities use the submitted requests and orders to help draw up their allocation plans.[33]

Wholesale organizations play an important part in planning the assortment and quality of goods. Since government plans cannot specify the output of goods in detail, matters of design, color, size, model, and similar variations are worked out among the organizations participating in the channel.[34]

In the satellite countries, state ownership and cooperative enterprises gradually have replaced private trading operations. In Poland, for example, almost 90 percent of the retail establishments were privately owned in 1946. By 1960, the private sector controlled only 12 percent of the stores, and these stores handled less than 3 percent of the total retail sales volume.[35] Of the balance, state stores handled nearly half the trade, with a slightly higher share going to cooperatives.

Rural cooperatives handle virtually all the nonprivate retail trade in country areas. These cooperatives operate as federations. Purchases are

[30] V. I. Gogol, "Wholesaling in the U.S.S.R." in Robert Bartels, *Comparative Marketing; Wholesaling in Fifteen Countries,* Richard D. Irwin, Inc., Homewood, Ill., 1963, pp. 227–250.
[31] Goldman, *op. cit.,* p. 25.
[32] Gogol, *op. cit.,* p. 237.
[33] Goldman, *op. cit.,* p. 56.
[34] Gogol, *op. cit.,* p. 231.
[35] J. Hart Walters, "Retailing in Poland; a First Hand Report," *Journal of Marketing* (April, 1964), pp. 16–21.

made partly from integrated wholesale establishments and partly from state wholesale organizations, state and cooperative factories, and agricultural sources.

Retail outlets in the cities include chains—mainly in food—operated by urban cooperatives; stores which are integrated with state-owned manufacturing enterprises; and state-owned stores which specialize in specific commodity fields.[36] Although there has been some growth in self-service retailing (especially in food), customers still shop in a variety of small, limited-line establishments.

The vertical control over distribution exercised by the state may be illustrated by the shoe industry of Hungary. The Central Planning Office, on the basis of past demand and the availability of resources, determines the number and types of shoes to be produced. Directives are forwarded to the shoe division of the Ministry of Light Industry and to the comparable division at the Ministry of Trade where the national shoe-store chain is located. The divisions then make contracts with the shoe factories and the national shoe-store chain. Shipments are made to the regional warehouses of the chain for allocation among the stores.[37]

Changes in Wholesale Structures

As changes occur in the retail structure, corresponding changes occur in wholesaling. Channels of distribution are likely to be longer in the less-developed countries, and two or more wholesalers may be used. As countries develop, the smaller wholesalers, especially of the subwholesale type, tend to be eliminated. The remaining wholesalers become larger and stronger except in fields where large-scale retailers buy directly from manufacturers. When the latter development occurs, wholesalers may establish voluntary chains, particularly in food and other convenience lines.

As was true in the United States, many wholesalers perform ineffectively from the manufacturer's point of view. Consequently, the poorer performers have been displaced by some manufacturers who sell directly to retailers. Where the wholesaler has been able to improve his operations, he has been able to regain his position in the channel.

---

[36] *Ibid.*
[37] Nicholas Bartsch, *East-Central Europe—A Comparative Market Survey* (unpublished).

German wholesalers, for example, have gone through this pattern. They had been in a weak position for several years prior to World War II. Manufacturers had established their own sales organizations or had sold through selling syndicates or brokers. In the postwar resurgence of Germany, wholesalers improved their managment practices and their services to both manufacturers and retailers. Also, specialized-function wholesalers appeared. Even so, there is some evidence that these changes have benefited a rather small number of wholesalers. More than one-third of the total wholesale volume is handled by less than one-half of one percent of the wholesalers, about five hundred enterprises.[38]

In Italy, which has one wholesaler for every ten retailers, manufacturers are tending to bypass wholesalers as a result of inadequate wholesaler service. Sales are made either by their own sales organizations or by agents. This development has occurred in such convenience goods as food and toiletries as well as in durable goods. As manufacturers shorten their channels, some wholesalers have shifted to imported goods or to discount-type retail operations.[39]

Dominance of the Wholesaler in Japan

Wholesalers have been a dominant part of the Japanese marketing system for several hundred years. After Japan was opened for trade with the West, the largest trading companies evolved into highly integrated Zaibatsu organizations, which included manufacturing plants, banking facilities, and wholesaling units. Wholesalers may actually control the distribution of certain industrial materials and consumer goods, and, in some cases, "put out" materials to processors. Although manufacturers have come to occupy a stronger place in marketing channels, wholesalers continue to be of major importance. In fact, a product may move through several wholesalers, as indicated by Figure 1.

> The use of a short channel is still unusual even in the case of large retail buyers . . . the use of long channels is the common practice for both industrial and consumer goods. The use of three or more wholesale links is not limited to very small firms. . . . The atomistic size of the large proportion of manufacturers, wholesalers, and retailers, plus their limited

[38] Robert Mieschlag, "Wholesaling in West Germany," in Bartels, *op. cit.,* pp. 10–20.
[39] Allvin, *op. cit.*

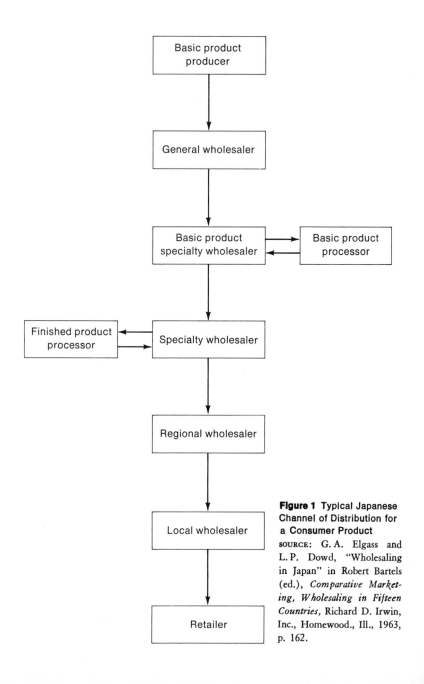

Figure 1 Typical Japanese Channel of Distribution for a Consumer Product

SOURCE: G. A. Elgass and L. P. Dowd, "Wholesaling in Japan" in Robert Bartels (ed.), *Comparative Marketing, Wholesaling in Fifteen Countries,* Richard D. Irwin, Inc., Homewood., Ill., 1963, p. 162.

capital encourages, if not requires, that the firms which perform the functions in the channel system make use of an additional link or two.[40]

In order to limit the growth of large-scale retailers in Japan, particularly department stores, special legislation was passed in the mid-fifties (the Department Store Law, June, 1956) to control the expansion of such stores. One result of this legislation has been to reduce the store space used for storage and to increase the space used for selling by shifting as much of the storage function as possible to the supplier.[41] As a consequence, since stores order in smaller quantities, they have become even more dependent on wholesalers than on manufacturers as a source of supply.

Marketing in Underdeveloped Countries

In the underdeveloped areas of the world, the typical retail institution is the market, or bazaar. These are often traveling markets. Those who participate in the market set up and dismantle their portable stalls daily. One writer, describing the markets of Nigeria, indicates that these markets, which often are shifted from one location to another, are the retail heart of the country:

> A good-sized market . . . may attract 5,000 sellers and as many as 25,000 to 100,000 customers in a single day . . . the great majority of market traders are women. . . . Most market traders specialize in a narrow line of products, for example, peppers, jewelry, enamelware, or cloth, but some will sell broader related lines such as soaps, medicines and cosmetics together. A trader's quantity of goods available is limited to what she can carry on her head or the distance she must walk to market, possibly with the assistance of her children. Thus, her stock is seldom large. Competition is extremely keen.[42]

Since it is customary for native African women to support themselves and perhaps their children by trading, they have become a dominant factor in retail and wholesale trade. They constitute a hierarchy of "mammy traders," ranging from those who do a sizable wholesale busi-

[40] G. A. Elgass, and L. P. Dowd, "Wholesaling in Japan," in Bartels, *op. cit.,* p. 163.
[41] Robert E. Weigand, "Department Stores in Japan," *Journal of Retailing* (Fall, 1963), pp. 31ff.
[42] Raymond W. Baker, "Marketing in Nigeria," *Journal of Marketing,* (July, 1965), pp. 40–48.

ness to the "penny mammy trader" in a local market, whose customers buy "one razor blade, two cigarettes, a handful of salt, three bananas, or a few tomatoes." [43] In West Africa, there are too many petty traders of this type. Several may participate in a single channel, with the result that the final prices may be more than three times the original cost.

Multiple wholesaling is common in underdeveloped areas. The largest wholesalers frequently are importers. They may sell to secondary wholesalers in outlying markets, who in turn sell to traders or retailers.

In India, trade is often looked upon as being unproductive. Therefore, manufacturers frequently avoid becoming engaged in marketing.[44] Sales are made through selling agents rather than through the manufacturer's own sales organization. Since agents may not sell aggressively, however, wholesale buyers may seek out merchandise through a broker. This is quite common among smaller wholesalers. Actually, the roles of Indian wholesalers are not clear-cut. Some may combine a merchant and agency business. Others, particularly subwholesalers, may operate at both wholesale and retail levels. The channels used for manufactured goods in India are shown in Figure 2.

One characteristic of wholesalers and traders in many underdeveloped areas is that they also buy the surplus production of the area:

> The petty retailer may not only sell his goods, but probably also buys raw produce from the farmers in the area—produce that will ultimately enter the export market. Sometimes these two functions merge into one transaction; the local customer barters his wares (ground nuts, for example) for cloth or hardware. Similarly, the wholesaler sells consumer goods to the petty retailer, and buys the latter's combined lots of farm produce, gathering the supplies of many such retailers into larger bundles. Ultimately, the large European firms will amass these bundles of produce—now reaching large quantities—and export them; they will also break down the bulk import purchases into smaller lots for sale to the wholesaler.[45]

The informal markets and bazaars of the older type may evolve into a more modern institution, as in South Africa, where chains of general-

---

[43] Mildred R. Marcus, "Merchandise Distribution in Tropical Africa," *Journal of Retailing* (Winter, 1959–69), pp. 197–201.

[44] Leon V. Hirsch, "Wholesaling in India," in Bartels, *op. cit.*, pp. 126ff.

[45] Edward Marcus, "Selling the Tropical African Market," *Journal of Marketing* (July, 1961), pp. 25–31.

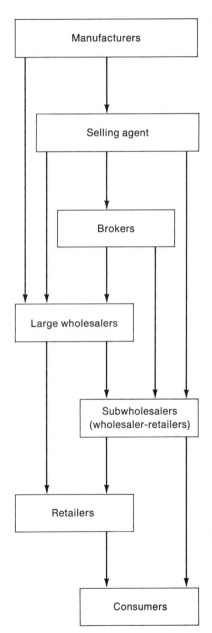

Figure 2 Distribution of Manufactured Goods in India

SOURCE: Leon V. Hirsch, "Wholesaling in India," in Robert Bartels (ed.), *Comparative Marketing, Wholesaling in Fifteen Countries,* Richard D. Irwin, Inc., Homewood, Ill., 1963, p. 136.

merchandise "bazaars" have become established. Self-service and other modern retailing devices may cause problems for native customers, however:

> . . . Many of the less-educated Africans find the system awkward to cope with because they have difficulty relating the cash in their pockets to the sum of goods they have bought. Many of them make a fresh circuit through the check-out turnstiles after each purchase to count their change.[46]

As in the earlier history of the United States, the general store is the most common retail institution in many underdeveloped areas. Sometimes these are "company stores," as in Brazil, where the *fazenda,* or plantation store, is found:

> Many *fazendas* employ as many as two thousand workers who live in small villages on the *fazenda.* In an effort to reduce prices for employees, the owners offer necessities through their own retail outlets. These are like large warehouses, stocking only the bare essentials. All purchases are on a credit basis, and the employee is never out of debt to the employer.[47]

One of the oldest retail institutions is the peddler, or hawker. Carson relates how the hawkers of tropical Africa

> . . . ply the streets of cities and towns on foot, crying out their wares, or they cycle from village to village, often following a regular route. They tend to concentrate on merchandise that has a high value to bulk, such as medicinal pills, toiletries, and small measures of tea, salt, and sugar.[48]

And in India:

> In the small villages, where most of the population lives, there are no retail shops. Individuals buy very little. Hawkers travel to villages, selling frequently purchased items such as utensils and cloth which they carry on their backs and heads. They often make exchanges by barter or partial payment. For special occasions such as a wedding, when the parents may give the bride and groom some household utensils, villagers will go to neighboring towns to buy.[49]

---

[46] "South African Retailing," *Economist* (Oct. 16, 1965), p. 318.

[47] Donald A. Taylor, "Retailing in Brazil," *Journal of Marketing* (July, 1959), pp. 54–58.

[48] David Carson, "Wholesaling in Tropical Africa," in Bartels, *op. cit.,* p. 191.

[49] Ralph Westfall and Harper W. Boyd, "Marketing in India," *Journal of Marketing* (October, 1960), p. 14.

An institution which is of major importance in some underdeveloped areas is the trading company. One of the largest is the United Africa Company, an affiliate of Unilever Ltd. This huge organization not only is engaged in exporting and importing in West Africa but operates plantations, processing plants for raw materials, and plants for manufacturing consumer goods. It purchases all of the region's basic raw materials for export or processing and operates wholesale and retail subsidiaries which handle a wide range of imported and local consumer products.[50]

---

[50] Carson, *op. cit.*

4

Control
of the
Channel
Network

Marketing may be explained in terms of a "flow" of goods and services; in fact, these flows can easily be traced out. It is a flow which is governed, however, not by natural forces, as the physical analogy might imply, but by a large number of factors related to the product, the market, the producer, and the available channels. The channel to be used in a particular case is, therefore, seldom a foregone choice.

The specific factors which are considered in channel choice will be discussed in Chapter 6. It may be pointed out here, however, that channel arrangements rest on negotiation between buyer and seller at each stage of the channel. No goods will move until there is agreement between the two parties covering such matters as product description, packaging, quantity involved, price, terms of sale, shipping quantities and dates, and services required. In both the industrial field and resale consumer goods, the producer will have to demonstrate a high degree of reliability.

In some instances, negotiations of this type are undertaken with respect to every sale. In other cases, once the basic arrangements have been determined, succeeding transactions follow the same pattern and are essentially of a routine nature.[1] For example, a considerable amount of negotiation will be involved in the infrequent purchase of a turbine-generator unit by a power-and-light company. If the product is pole-

[1] See Wroe Alderson, *Marketing Behavior and Executive Action*, Richard D. Irwin, Inc., Homewood, Ill., 1957, chap. 5, for a discussion of negotiation in marketing channels.

line hardware, however, the major sales effort is related to getting on the utility's list of approved suppliers. Once on the list, the supplier can expect to receive orders with very little negotiation. Likewise, a mail-order-house buyer may negotiate at length to select items to be placed in the catalog. As customer orders are received, routine orders are placed with the supplier for inventory replacement.

Routine transactions are continued, of course, only as long as the arrangement is satisfactory to both parties. Their only purpose is to introduce greater efficiency into distribution, not greater rigidity. Whenever new channel opportunities appear, those who stand to gain are likely to examine them carefully.

The process of negotiation involves power relationships, and generally the parties are unequal in strength. Furthermore, shifts in the relative strength of the parties in a channel occur over time. Prior to the Civil War, in the United States, the wholesaler was typically the dominant factor in the channel. Small retailers, and frequently small manufacturers as well, depended on the wholesaler to carry stocks and to give credit or financial support. Following the Civil War, large-scale retailers became the dominant element in the distribution of convenience goods and certain shopping goods.

As manufacturers have grown larger and as oligopolistic conditions have prevailed in many industries, the manufacturer has held a position of strength in the channel. Nevertheless, at times this has meant a large manufacturer facing a large-scale retailer. Under such circumstances, the point of major strength may be indeterminant, but it is likely to lie with the retailer. This is illustrated particularly by the abuses which have arisen in the use of cooperative advertising allowances by some large retailers.

The manufacturer, even the largest, is likely to feel dependent on his retail outlets. Ordinarily, he cannot displace the retailer, whereas the retailer will usually have access to comparable merchandise. This allows the retailer to make various demands on the manufacturer and to secure the manufacturer's compliance.

In a few instances, the user may occupy the dominant position. This may occur under conditions of oligopsony, where a market consists of a few industrial buyers. The food industry is a case in point. A limited number of packers, sometimes only one, may be operating in a producing area, and the grower's alternatives for sale are severely limited.

Dominance in a channel, in the sense of negotiating power, can be the result of product and service differentiation, financial resources, volume of sales or purchases, geographical advantage, the ability to integrate forward or backward, and limited competition.

The other countries of the world have not experienced the retail-dominated market-power structure which has existed in the United States. This is primarily because large-scale retailers have been of limited importance, and even where they are found, they tend not to be so aggressive as United States' firms. There are examples of domination by wholesalers in some countries, however, such as Japan.

Balance between Conflict and Cooperation in the Channel

In the sense that the units in a channel of distribution are performing a common service (i.e., they are engaged in the joint effort of getting the goods produced into the possession of the user), they are "cooperating" through specialization of labor. At a given point in time, with respect to a particular product, each member of the channel is doing that part of the job which he can do best. For the moment, the channel may be said to be in equilibrium. In economies which are in the lower stages of market development, such a state of equilibrium may last for many years. In highly dynamic economies such as the United States, however, manufacturers and middlemen are constantly testing the balance and are either taking on or dropping the performance of certain functions. Some examples of these shifts and the reasons for them will be presented later in the chapter.

Channel Conflicts

Conflict in the channel may be created by either the producer of the product or the middlemen who sell it. Manufacturers may create conflict and upset the channel balance by such actions as selling to a middleman's customers, thus competing directly with him; by making heavy demands on middlemen, such as requiring large and varied inventories, special promotional support, extensive service facilities, burdensome payment terms, etc.; by refusing to protect middlemen against model changes and price changes; by making goods available to a middleman's competitors, perhaps to firms of a different type; and by various other requirements and harassments. Manufacturers who are not satisfied with the existing channel situation and the performance of middlemen will adopt appropriate measures to increase their market share and improve long-run profitability.

Middlemen, especially large-scale retailers, can create conflict by demanding large discounts, special promotional allowances, and more favorable pricing terms. They may also demand special shipping arrangements, quicker deliveries, protection against price changes, etc. Clearly, such demands on either side are a show of strength and a sign that the potential gains from conflict are greater than continued cooperation along previously established lines.

Each party in the channel will examine the channel arrangements in terms of his own interests. If alternatives are available which offer greater profit probabilities at a bearable risk, a change in channel policies of the conflict type is likely to be initiated. If satisfactory alternatives are not available, manufacturers particularly may look for ways to make existing relationships more profitable on a mutual basis.

For the most part, large-scale retailers have chosen to embark on programs which involve some degree of conflict with suppliers. Exceptions to this have been those instances where retailers have been willing to cooperate with manufacturers on an exclusive, limited-outlet basis or where they have encouraged and worked closely with certain small suppliers, as have the general-mail-order houses.

Wholesalers have tended to enhance their position by strengthening their retail customers. As will be noted below, this may take the form of establishing voluntary chains. Somewhat indirectly, wholesalers may adopt tactics of conflict by withdrawing as a supplier of nonaffiliated retailers. Usually, wholesalers have gone to great length to cooperate with supplying manufacturers, often when it might have been more profitable to reduce the number of competing brands carried.

Some of the closest working relationships have developed between manufacturers and their agents, especially selling agents. In these instances, the agent may serve as an extension of the manufacturers' own sales organization. Where there is mutual confidence between the parties, the relationship may be close and of long standing.

Wholesalers of agricultural products, especially commission houses, have, at times, been in conflict with producers and have not always served them well. They have benefited from a monopoly buying position in some instances and in others have taken advantage of the producer's lack of price information.

On the sales side, large consumer goods' manufacturers of well-known brands quite commonly adopt policies of conflict, such as selling direct to retailers and making excessive demands on both wholesalers and retailers. Automobile manufacturers may make very heavy demands on dealers but at the same time may engage in various activities intended to aid the dealer. Manufacturers of industrial products may sell in competition with wholesale middlemen, but some work very closely with their distributors, particularly in training the distributor's sales and service employees.

On the supply side, processors may squeeze suppliers. However, some processors supply the material and the knowledge needed to produce a high-quality product. Canners, for example, develop special strains which are supplied to growers.

In summary, producers and middlemen continually review the channel options available to them. On both the supply and the sales side, possible shifts toward greater conflict or greater cooperation are evaluated. It is this process of continuous evaluation which brings about improvements and greater efficiency in channels of distribution. However, regardless of the relative strength of the parties in a channel, they are engaged in the exploitation of a joint opportunity, the opportunity to handle the distribution of some particular product. And, in some manner, the functions to be performed are divided among them.

Methods of Securing Channel Control

Manufacturers have adopted several methods to extend their control over distribution beyond the immediate sale. One of these is to engage in selective distribution. This involves selecting one wholesale or retail middleman in an area—i.e., exclusive distribution—or, alternatively, selling to a limited number of outlets.

This device enhances the manufacturer's control over the next link in the channel in several ways. He can expect the middleman to carry complete stocks, give effective promotional support, follow suggested pricing practices, and perform the necessary service activities. He cannot, however, usually dictate the geographical area to be covered by the middleman, and he may encounter difficulty in attempting to dictate the types of customers to be served. Nevertheless, the manufacturer can exercise considerable control over the resale of his products by this device, although this control should not impinge too heavily on the prerogatives of middlemen.

The concept of joint opportunity still holds under this relationship. If the product line is one which is sought by middlemen, the manufacturer can expect compliance with his policies as one condition for retaining the franchise. But if the terms are too onerous, the "opportunity" is no longer attractive to middlemen.

Selective distribution policies are used at the wholesale level by a wide range of manufacturers of both consumer and industrial products. At the retail level, these policies are used primarily for specialty goods (such as high-priced apparel), sometimes for shopping goods (for example, furniture), rarely for convenience goods (gasoline is an exception).

Over the years, and especially since World War II, the concept of selective distribution has been extended to the franchise system of distribution. Under this arrangement, an entrepreneur typically develops the operating plans for a type of business in considerable detail. The business may involve the sale of a line of products (usually to the ultimate consumer) or a consumer or business service. The franchiser makes available a "package" which includes the entire operating system, lists of necessary equipment and materials, and, frequently, building plans.

Franchisers of drive-in eating facilities, for example, have developed elaborate operating systems. These include guidance in selecting a location, complete blueprints and floor plans, model inventories, guidance in financing, centralized purchasing of equipment, supplies, and resale items; operating manuals, central planning and implementation of promotional activities, guidance in pricing, tested record-keeping and tax systems, and employee training. The franchisee furnishes capital, initiative, and, preferably, some business experience. The franchiser furnishes nearly everything else.

In order to retain the franchise, the franchisee must follow the franchise terms and operating procedures carefully, often to the letter.[2] The control exercised by the franchiser accomplishes two purposes: (1) It

[2] For a discussion of franchising procedures and controls see Edwin H. Lewis and Robert S. Hancock, *The Franchise System of Distribution,* School of Business Administration, University of Minnesota, Minneapolis, 1963.

enables people with no experience in the field, and perhaps with little or no business experience of any kind, to operate a business successfully. (2) It provides for a degree of standardization in operations which increases public acceptance and patronage and thus leads to greater success and profitability for the whole venture.[3]

Integration

The greatest degree of control over distribution is achieved through forward integration. Manufacturers may establish wholesale and/or retail outlets which will handle the manufacturer's line and, sometimes, allied lines of other manufacturers as well. The manufacturer, thereby, can control distribution either to the retailer or all the way to the consumer.

Manufacturers may also integrate backward toward the sources of raw materials and semimanufactures. And producers of semifinished goods may occasionally integrate forward to later stages of the manufacturing process.

By maintaining ownership of more than one level of activity, the manufacturer automatically performs the necessary distribution functions and can secure maximum control over the marketing mix. There are various reasons why manufacturers move in the direction of integration, and there are certain circumstances which enable firms to integrate successfully.

One author tested some fifteen variables which appear to influence vertical integration in specific industries. He found that the following factors seemed to be of major importance:

A. Factors external to the channel system
  1. The threat posed by a competing system—If vertical integration is undertaken successfully by one channel, competing channels are under pressure to integrate also.
  2. A change in market conditions—As new market segments, new products, and new product uses appear, marketing problems are created which may best be solved through integration.

[3] Most franchise businesses are regional or national in scope, and each operating unit is expected to give support to the basic franchise image. The 1966 edition of *Franchise Annual,* published by *National Franchise Reports,* Chicago, lists more than 650 franchising organizations.

B. Factors internal to the channel system
  1. The presence of firms with a broad market base which permits them to integrate profitably.
  2. The existence of channel conflicts, particularly with sources of supply.
  3. The presence of aggressive innovators in the system who are willing to try new channel arrangements.[4]

Other significant factors included were (1) an optimistic economic outlook, (2) a favorable legal environment, (3) the acceptance of vertical integration as a form of marketing strategy, (4) an opportunity to expand profits by performing tasks presently handled by others, (5) duplication in the performance of functions in the present system, (6) attempts to secure better utilization of a firm's resources, (7) the financial ability to undertake integration.

During the postwar period (1948–1963), sales of manufacturers' stock-carrying branches increased more rapidly than sales of merchant wholesalers in several commodity lines, including machinery and equipment, lumber and millwork, certain paper products, amusement and sporting goods, drugs, footwear, electrical appliances, and hardware.[5] Actual dollar sales of merchant wholesalers are substantially larger than sales of manufacturers' branches in the above categories, except for industrial machinery and footwear; and the number of establishments is very much larger for merchant wholesalers in each of these lines.

The growth in manufacturers' branch sales appears to reflect a desire to have stocks readily available in the field, in order to give rapid delivery and particularly to meet delivery schedules of competitors who have taken the lead in establishing field stocks. In many cases, such stocks probably constitute backup stocks for wholesalers. Where wholesalers have not carried full inventories, particularly of slower-selling items, these regional manufacturer-stocks permit prompt delivery. Stock-carrying branches thus are a competitive selling device, especially for manufacturers who produce a broad line.

[4] Frederick D. Sturdivant, "Determinants of Vertical Integration in Channel Systems," in *Science Technology and Marketing,* American Marketing Association, Chicago, 1967.
[5] U.S. Bureau of the Census, *Census of Business, Wholesale Trade, United States Summary,* 1948 and 1963.

Voluntary Chains

During the early years of this country's growth, channels of distribution were often dominated by large wholesalers. They sold the output of comparatively small domestic manufacturers; and in a period when much merchandise originated abroad they were large-scale importers. Their dominance of trade channels was challenged first by manufacturers and later by the large-scale retailers. Not only was their dominance challenged, the functions they performed were gradually usurped, as well.

Caught in this kind of pincer movement, wholesalers sought to strengthen their position, and one of the solutions to their problem was the voluntary chain. The wholesaler-sponsored voluntary chain of the type found in groceries, hardware, automotive products, and variety lines enables the wholesaler to devise and implement a combined system of wholesale-retail operations which introduces both standardization and greater efficiency into the retail phase of the operation particularly. The wholesaler develops guidelines for virtually every phase of store operation and through field representatives works closely with retail members to ensure that recommended procedures are being followed. The voluntary chain, in fact, has much the same advantages for a retailer as are found in franchise organizations in other fields.

Many voluntary chains have been spectacularly successful. Not only do they have a strong influence on retail operations, but through their buying power—both for manufacturers' brands and their own—they have achieved a status at least equivalent to that of centrally owned chains, department store groups, and general-mail-order houses.

The small retailer, located at the end of the channel and subjected to pressures from manufacturers, wholesalers, and large-scale retail competitors, also found a way to raise his status in the channel. This was to combine with other retailers, form a central buying organization, and integrate backward by establishing what, in effect, is a wholesale organization. The first efforts in this direction resulted in loosely organized buying clubs or pools. Subsequently, formally organized retailer cooperatives, modeled somewhat along the lines of the wholesaler-sponsored voluntary chain, were established. Some of these, in the drug field particularly, were formed before the turn of the century.

Retailer cooperatives commonly put their greatest emphasis on the advantages of group buying and give less attention to retail management aids and services than do wholesaler-sponsored chains. Their primary objective, consequently, has been to attain some degree of dominance in the channel and to secure the buying advantages which had accrued to their chain and cooperative-affiliated competitors. The retailer becomes, in effect, his own wholesale buyer. So strong have the pressures toward the formation of large-scale buying groups been, in some areas, that very few unaffiliated retailers remain in such convenience goods as groceries, drugs, and hardware.

What impact does this quest for power and dominance in the channel have on the consumer? If he is a large industrial buyer, he may be able to retain considerable leverage in the market. He is not concerned with strong wholesale and retail organizations, since he does not buy from them. If his suppliers are as large as he is, or larger, the power relationship vis-à-vis his suppliers may be indeterminate and may fluctuate with market conditions. If his suppliers are typically small, he will normally play the dominant role. However, even here, where agricultural products are being purchased, producers may organize into marketing cooperatives.

The householder is usually considered to be rather helpless in this struggle for channel dominance. As an individual, he is no match for those engaged in the distribution of goods; but the cooperative device is also available to him, as it is to his suppliers. The consumer cooperative can function as a retail organization, and when formed into a federation can operate as a wholesaler and perhaps engage in processing and manufacturing as well.

In the last century, consumer cooperatives became important in the British Isles and in Northern and Central Europe. Because marketing services for consumer goods were poorly performed by existing agencies, there was an opportunity for consumers to band together in order to determine whether they could perform the retail—and later, wholesale—functions better. Frequently, it developed that they could, and so they created a new niche in trade channels.

In the United States, however, the evolutionary developments of trade channels were such that the shifting power structure resulted in greater efficiencies from which the consumer benefited. There was, consequently, no great need for the consumer to become more dominant in the channel, and except for a few areas where the ethnic background of the population created some interest in cooperatives, this institution has not secured a foothold in distribution channels.

Channel Efficiency

The changing patterns of channel dominance outlined above resulted from the efforts of units in the channel to shift the performance of some of the distribution functions. These shifts occurred when a given unit believed there was a better way of accomplishing certain distribution tasks. If the innovation, in fact, did result in the desired services being performed at lower cost, the change became an established feature of the channel. The struggle for control of particular segments of a channel springs from a desire to maximize organizational profits, but as long as alternative methods continue to be available and entrepreneurs are willing to bear the risk of attempting to make them work, only those patterns will survive which stand the test of time; and the final test is overall channel efficiency. The only justifiable channel system in our economy is one which performs the needed functions at lowest cost as compared with the recognized—and, presumably, tested—alternatives.

In practice, channel changes have come about through trial and error. Entrepreneurs experiment with new channel arrangements as new markets are developed, new products are added, greater financial resources become available, and more marketing experience and knowledge are gained. Thus, a manufacturer may decide to open a wholesale branch or to shift from agents to his own salesmen in some areas; a wholesaler may establish the nucleus of a voluntary chain; and a group of retailers may start to engage in joint buying. The resulting effect on corporate profits (assuming other channels are available) determines whether the change will be perpetuated.

Recently, researchers have turned to simulation procedures to study the movement of goods through trade channels. Simulation models can be constructed which show how goods will flow through designated channels in accordance with certain basic assumptions as to inventory requirements, frequency and size of orders, transportation and order-filling time, etc. Such a model would enable participants in the channel to devise an optimum flow of goods to fit specified conditions. By attaching costs to the commodity flow and introducing a price structure, the probable payoffs of alternative decisions can be calculated.[6]

Governmental Controls over Trade-channel Relationships

Business firms are precluded from making trade-channel arrangements or decisions which lessen competition, act as an unreasonable restraint on trade, or tend to create a monopoly. The underlying Federal legislation in these areas is contained in the Sherman Act (Sections 1 and 2) and the Clayton Act (Section 3 of the 1914 Act and Section 7, the Anti-merger Act of 1950). In addition, the Federal Trade Commission is empowered to act under Section 5 of the Federal Trade Commission Act of 1914 in cases where trade-channel activities constitute unfair methods of competition.

Some of the basic legal difficulties related to channels arise out of business mergers, either horizontal or vertical mergers involving forward or backward integration. During recent years, many mergers have been labeled "conglomerate" or, to use a term favored by the Federal Trade Commission, "product-extension" mergers. These are mergers which extend product offerings into new, although perhaps related, fields. Horizontal mergers are assumed to involve competitors in the same geographical market. The Federal Trade Commission is using the term "market-extension" merger as one which involves "firms which, while they sold the same product, were not actually competitors at the time of the merger since they sold in different geographical markets." [7]

When competitors merge, or even when companies producing allied lines merge, the Department of Justice or the Federal Trade Commission may see in the action a threat to competition. If channels which had been competitive or potentially competitive are merged, the resulting concentration of marketing power may not be considered to be in the public interest. This concern is particularly great if the companies are large and have well-known brands. Thus, the Federal Trade Commission issued divestiture orders against General Foods Corp. in con-

[6] For an application of simulation procedures to distribution channels see Stanley F. Stasch, "The Stability of Channel Systems: Two Dynamic Models," in *Science, Technology, and Marketing,* American Marketing Association, Chicago, 1967; also, the same author's unpublished dissertation, "A Method of Dynamically Analyzing the Stability of the Economic Structure of Channels of Distribution."

[7] Beatrice Foods Co., No. 6653, FTC, April, 1965.

nection with the acquisition of S.O.S. (scouring pad) products, and also against Procter and Gamble in connection with the acquisition of the Clorox Chemical Company.[8] In both situations the Commission was concerned with the enhanced marketing power and market position which could, and apparently did, result from acquiring these well-established brands.

In a major court case (Lever Brothers) involving the acquisition of the Monsanto detergent All, the Court took a different view.[9] It held that since All is a low-sudsing, heavy-duty detergent, it reached a special market segment or "submarket" of the detergent field and, consequently, did not directly parallel other heavy-duty detergents. Because of its marketing organization for household products, Lever was in a better position than Monsanto to make All a more effective competitor in the market.

The "submarket" concept was also a significant facet of the Brown Shoe case. The United States Supreme Court pointed out that it is necessary to determine the probable effect of a merger in each "economically significant submarket" in order to learn whether the merger will substantially lessen competition in any line of commerce under the terms of Section 7 of the Clayton Act. Under Section 7, it must be shown that the merger will substantially lessen competition or tend to create a monopoly. In the Brown Shoe case, the courts interpreted these clauses quite broadly. Although both companies (Brown Shoe Company and G. R. Kinney Company) had a small share of the market, the courts were concerned with an incipient threat to the competitive structure of the industry. The district court ordered the divestiture of Kin-

---

[8] General Foods Corporation, No. 8600 FTC, 1966.

The Procter and Gamble Company, No. 6901, FTC, 1963. The divestiture order covering Clorox was reversed by the Sixth Circuit Court of Appeals on the basis that postacquisition evidence did not show any anticompetitive effects resulting from the merger. The Supreme Court, however, in April, 1967, upheld the FTC divestiture order. Referring to the bases for the circuit court's .decision, the Supreme Court emphasized the need to judge the potential impact of mergers on markets. "Section 7 of the Clayton Act was intended to arrest the anticompetitive effects of market power in their incipiency. The core question is whether a merger may substantially lessen competition, and necessarily requires a prediction of the merger's impact on competition, present and future. . . . The section can deal only with probabilities, not with certainties. . . . And there is certainly no requirement that the anticompetitive power manifest itself in anticompetitive action before § 7 can be called into play."

[9] *United States v. Lever Brothers Company and Monsanto Chemical Company*, 216 F. Supp. 887 (1963).

ney and was upheld by the Supreme Court.[10] In light of the Supreme Court decision, it is apparent that companies which want to open or protect certain channels by taking the merger route may be vulnerable to charges under Section 7, even where the merger would fall far short of dominating the industry or where the probable impact would fall essentially on a particular product line or section of the country.

Exclusive Distribution Arrangements

Manufacturers may desire to secure greater control over trade channels by entering into exclusive distribution arrangements of various types with wholesale or retail middlemen. Exclusive arrangements are not illegal per se, but a number of major court cases have dealt with problems that have arisen in connection with them. Several of these actions have occurred in petroleum products.

The Federal Trade Commission has opposed the sales-commission agreements which have been made between some of the large oil companies and supplier manufacturers of auto accessories, particularly tires. Under these agreements, the suppliers pay the oil companies a commission on sales of these products to service stations. The United States Supreme Court, in one key case (Atlantic Refining), upheld the Federal Trade Commission on the grounds that the oil companies have considerable economic leverage over their service stations through the cancellation provisions of their station leases and equipment-loan contracts.[11] The Court viewed this as a restraint on competition at three levels: (1) manufacturers and wholesalers of other brands of tires were effectively closed out of the Atlantic service-station market; (2) since Atlantic had a similar arrangment with Firestone in another segment of the market, neither Firestone nor Goodyear could sell in markets allocated to the other; (3) Atlantic distributors and service stations had to compete with other middlemen who stocked multiple brands.

[10] *Brown Shoe Company, Inc., v. United States*, 370 U.S. 294 (1962).

Brown Shoe Company, Inc., v. United States, 82 Sup. Ct. 1502 (June, 1962).

The Brown Shoe Company merged with G. R. Kinney Company in 1956. Brown was primarily a manufacturer (fourth largest in the country). Kinney was basically a retailer and operated the largest chain of family shoe stores, with over 400 stores in some 270 cities. Since both companies operated manufacturing and retailing facilities, however, the case involved aspects of both a horizontal and vertical merger.

[11] *The Atlantic Refining Co. v. FTC; The Goodyear Tire and Rubber Co. v. FTC*, 85 Sup. Ct. 1498 (June, 1965).

There were two dissenting opinions to this decision which raise some question as to whether attacking the sales-commission plans gets to the root of the problem; but it is clear that companies which use contractual arrangements of this type to coerce middlemen—or which appear to do so—are vulnerable to government action.

Another type of economic leverage is found in the so-called tying arrangement (a situation in which a particular product will not be sold unless the purchaser accepts one or more additional products or services). In order to secure the most desired items, buyers may be required to purchase others that are less desired, and perhaps must purchase the entire line. The latter practice is known as "full-line forcing." Tying arrangements limit the range of choice of the purchaser, and the United States Supreme Court has held that such tying clauses are illegal where they serve to restrain trade substantially in the tied product or where they arise because of a monopoly position that the seller holds.[12]

Territorial Restrictions

Exclusive territorial arrangements, whereby middlemen are expected to confine their sales activities to residents of their assigned territories, have frequently come under court scrutiny. The Sixth Circuit Court of Appeals, in a case involving the Sandura Company (floor coverings), ruled that the firm's closed-territory system of distribution could not be considered unfair competition as claimed by the Federal Trade Commission. The court held that the system was justifiable in terms of the competitive situation facing the company and that it was needed to get the necessary support from distributors. The court found no evidence of horizontal conspiracy.[13]

In a similar case involving Snap-on Tools, the Seventh Circuit Court of Appeals concluded that assigned exclusive territories actually aided interbrand competition, and that there was no indication of a conspiracy that would restrict horizontal competition.[14] The agreement also contained a provision whereby the company reserved for itself certain industrial accounts. The court found no objection to this, stating, in

[12] *Times-Picayune Publishing Co. v. United States,* 345 U.S. 594, 608–609 (1953); *Northern Pacific Railway Co. v. United States,* 356 U.S. 1, 6 (1958).
[13] *Sandura Co. v. FTC* (6th Cir. December, 1964).
[14] *Snap-on Tools Corp. v. FTC* (7th Cir. July, 1963).

effect, that dealers would not ordinarily have the facilities or the competence to handle this business satisfactorily.

In 1963, the Supreme Court remanded a case involving the White Motor Co. to the district court and instructed the court to determine the economic and business implications of the company's territorial restrictions.[15] In 1967, however, in the Schwinn bicycle case, the Court ruled against Schwinn's practice of restricting territories and customers served by wholesalers.[16] The majority opinion stated, "If a manufacturer parts with dominion over his product or transfers the risk to another, he may not reserve control over its destiny or the condition of resale." The Court added, however, that its ruling did not apply to consignment arrangements with middlemen.

Another significant case was concerned with the arrangement under which bedding manufacturers were licensed to manufacture and sell in an exclusive territory under the Sealy brand name.[17] The district court had held that the system of exclusive regional licensees used by Sealy was an effective way to achieve maximum market development and found no evidence that the system was developed for the purpose of protecting the markets of licensees or for eliminating competition among them. When the case reached the Supreme Court, however, the Court decided that the arrangements among regional manufacturers and Sealy were essentially horizontal rather than vertical, since Sealy was controlled by the regional franchise holders. Consequently, the effect was one of collusion and restraint of trade in which territorial restrictions were combined with "unlawful price fixing and policing." [18] This decision puts companies on notice that the Court will not accept arrangements which purport to be vertical in nature but are actually devised by regional entities with horizontal competitive relationships.

Franchise Arrangements

The post-World War II period has seen the extensive development of franchise systems. Franchise agreements frequently specify in some detail

---

[15] *The White Motor Co. v. United States,* 83 Sup. Ct. 696 (1963). In 1964, the case was settled by consent judgment in which the company agreed not to restrict the territories or the customers of distributors and dealers. (N.D. Ohio, September, 1964.)

[16] *Arnold Schwinn and Co. v. United States,* 388 Sup. Ct. 365 (June, 1967).

[17] *United States v. Sealy Incorporated,* N.D. Ill. (October, 1964).

[18] *United States v. Sealy Incorporated,* 388 Sup. Ct. 350 (June, 1967).

how the business is to be conducted and may place certain restrictions on the franchisee. Franchisees of the Brown Shoe Company, for example, were expected not to handle competing lines in return for services furnished without charge by the company, including services of field representatives, training programs, merchandising and record-keeping systems, and group purchase of insurance. The Federal Trade Commission issued a cease and desist order concerning the use of such franchise agreements on the basis that they constituted an unfair trade practice under Section 5 of the Federal Trade Commission Act. The position of the Commission was that these arrangements prevented other manufacturers from selling to this bloc of retail outlets.

The appellate court set aside the FTC order on the grounds that the company did not have a monopoly of the services offered. Other manufacturers provided similar services, and retailers were free to drop the Brown line and add another if they wished. The services involved, therefore, could not be considered a "tying" arrangement used to coerce dealers in making purchases from Brown.[19] The case went to the Supreme Court, and the Court sided with the Commission.[20] The Court held that the Commission under Section 5 of the Federal Trade Commission Act does *not* have to prove that franchise agreements may "substantially lessen competition or tend to create a monopoly." As a result of this decision, the FTC is given additional support in its efforts to take action against trade restraints under the provisions of Section 5.

Some California automobile dealers began selling through discount houses and referral services. General Motors attempted to halt this practice under the terms of its contract with Chevrolet dealers. The Department of Justice contended that such action by General Motors constituted restraint of trade under Section 1 of the Sherman Act. The district court disagreed and indicated that the franchise system, as set up, provided for the orderly marketing of automobiles and furnished the customer services necessary to maintain goodwill for General Motors' cars. An open method of competition of the type envisioned by the Department of Justice would not, in the court's view, be desirable.[21] In 1967, the Supreme Court reversed the district court by calling the ac-

---

[19] *Brown Shoe Co., Inc., v. FTC* (8th Cir. December, 1964).

[20] *FTC v. Brown Shoe Co., Inc.*, 86 Sup. Ct. 1501 (June, 1966).

[21] *United States v. General Motors Corp., Losor Chevrolet Dealers Association, Dealers Service, Inc., and Foothill Dealer's Association* (S.D. Cal. September, 1964).

tions of General Motors and its dealers a conspiracy in restraint of trade by attempting to prevent price cutting.[22] Decisions of this type tend to give support to discount houses and other retailers who sell on the basis of price appeal.

Manufacturers and others who operate franchise systems retain the right to terminate the franchise for cause. However, the termination prerogative cannot be a device for coercion of the franchisee, nor can it be used as a method to restrain trade. In a case involving Sinclair Refining Company, the Fourth Circuit Court of Appeals pointed out that there are limitations to a seller's right to "refuse to deal." If this right is used to maintain a situation which violates antitrust legislation, those injured are entitled to triple damages under the Clayton Act.[23]

A franchisee cannot claim damages, however, when a franchise is terminated under conditions where there is no evidence of "coercion, intimidation, or threats of coercion or intimidation." [24] The franchiser, in effect, is under no obligation to renew a franchise after it expires if he does not wish to do so.

Reciprocity

Business firms which are in a dominant position relative to their suppliers of goods or services may bring pressure on these suppliers to purchase from them. The Federal Trade Commission and the Department of Justice have become increasingly concerned with reciprocity arrangements. The Federal Trade Commission has issued cease and desist orders in situations where coercive reciprocity arrangements appeared to exist; and in recent cases, the Department of Justice has requested divestiture of corporate divisions where it appeared that reciprocity was a calculated part of the merger. In two instances, among others, one involving the sale of electric locomotives and the other the sale of carbon dioxide to corporate suppliers, the corporations were charged with exercising their buying power to build sales of corporate divisions making the products indicated.[25]

[22] *United States v. General Motors Corp. et al.,* 86 Sup. Ct. 1321 (April, 1966).

[23] *S. Kriete Osborn v. Sinclair Refining Company* (4th Cir. November, 1963).

[24] *Berry Brothers Buick, Inc., v. General Motors Corporation (Buick Division)* (E.D. Pa. August, 1966).

[25] *United States v. General Motors Corporation,* Civil Action 63C 80 (Jan. 14, 1963).
  United States v. General Dynamics Corporation, Civil Action 62C 3686 (Nov. 8,

The Federal government appears to be broadening its attack on corporate reciprocity arrangements. In a suit filed in March, 1967, against General Tire and Rubber Co. and three of its subsidiaries—Aerojet-General Corp., RKO-General, Inc., and A. M. Byers Co.—the Department of Justice seems to be attempting to establish the principle that any systematic program of securing reciprocal trade agreements from suppliers violates the antitrust laws even though no coercion is involved. If the courts accept this viewpoint, many existing reciprocity agreements will be challenged.

The current position of the Supreme Court may be found in the unanimous opinion given in the Consolidated Foods case. Consolidated Foods had purchased Gentry, Inc., a producer of dehydrated onions and garlic. Eleven years after the purchase, the Federal Trade Commission ruled that the merger was in violation of Section 7 of the Clayton Act, since it gave Consolidated the "power to extort or simply attract reciprocal purchases from suppliers . . . (and) to foreclose competition from a substantial share of the markets for dehydrated onion and garlic." The court of appeals reversed the Commission's decision on the grounds that ten years of experience under the merger indicated that the conditions feared by the Commission had not materialized.[26]

The Supreme Court, however, reversed the circuit court and upheld the Commission.[27] The Court said that if postacquisition evidence were to be "given conclusive weight or was allowed to override all probabilities, then acquisition would go forward willy-nilly, the parties biding their time until reciprocity was allowed fully to bloom." And further, ". . . Section 7 of the Clayton Act is concerned with probabilities not certainties. Reciprocity in trading as a result of an acquisition violates Section 7, if the probability of a lessening of competition is shown."

Quite clearly reciprocity arrangements are going to be more closely scrutinized by government agencies and there is every indication that the Supreme Court will hold to its present view that reciprocity is "one

---

1962). In 1966, the District Court of Southern New York ordered the divestiture of the Liquid Carbonic Division of General Dynamics. The court held that reciprocity contracts are similar to "tying" clauses which have been held to be per se violations of Section 1 of the Sherman Act where the sales volume involved is "not insubstantial."

[26] *Consolidated Foods Corp. v.* FTC (7th Cir. March, 1964).

[27] *FTC v. Consolidated Foods Corp.,* 85 Sup. Ct. 1220 (April, 1965).

of the congeries of anticompetitive practices at which the antitrust laws are aimed." [28]

Furthermore, in recent cases, the Supreme Court has supported the concept of "incipient anticompetitive effects." In refusing to base its decisions on actual "market experience," as the lower courts have done in several cases, the Court has indicated clearly that any company action which gives evidence of having substantial anticompetitive repercussions in the future should be examined for possible antitrust violations.

[28] *Ibid.*

5

Distribution
Policies

Channel systems come into being as the result of decisions made by sellers and buyers concerning the market contacts to be made and the sources of supply to be used. In the very great majority of market transactions, alternatives are available to buyers and sellers at all levels.

Distribution policy is one aspect of a firm's marketing mix, and such policies, consequently, become part of the firm's marketing strategy. The manufacturer, for example, needs to decide to what extent it is desirable and possible to control the distribution of his products. At the one extreme, a manufacturer of standardized electrical wire and cable may decide to turn all selling activities over to manufacturers' agents. In such a case, the manufacturer's control is limited primarily to the selection and reassignment of agents. It is likely that he will be able to exercise very little authority over agents' operations. Conversely, a manufacturer of industrial machinery, for reasons which will be indicated below, will probably deal directly with the user of the machinery and so control distribution to the point of use.

Middlemen, too, especially wholesalers, have distribution policies. They may decide to sell to a particular segment of the market such as institutional buyers, repair shops, or contractors. And buyers, including the ultimate consumer, also make decisions regarding their sources of supply.

Distribution policies fall into three categories: (1) those related to the level of contact or depth of channel penetration, e.g., agent, distributor, retailer, or user, (2) those related to the scope of distribution, i.e., general distribution or some form of selective distribution, and (3) those related to the choice of specific firms to handle the line.

Manufacturers' Distribution Policies

A manufacturer's distribution policy relates initially to the degree to which he wishes to exercise control over distribution and the depth to which he wishes to penetrate the market with his own personnel. The greatest degree of market penetration involves direct sale to users. This occurs rather infrequently in consumers' goods but is used by some manufacturers of specialty-type goods whose marketing strategy rests on the appeal of "buying direct" from the manufacturer. Contact with the customer may be made by the manufacturer's sales force or by what is technically an agency organization. Manufacturers of household brushes, cookware, cosmetics, apparel, books, and specialty food products, among others, have used this approach to customers. Some manufacturers of apparel, shoes, and sporting goods sell by direct mail through the use of catalogs. Retail stores are operated by some well-known manufacturers of shoes, apparel, confectionery, automobile supplies, paper specialties, and household equipment.

Manufacturers who sell directly to consumers base their marketing strategy on the specialty-product concept. Quality and product uniqueness, completeness of line, and specialty selling services (such as display) are typically emphasized, although convenience and implied lower costs are often added appeals. In effect, these manufacturers are taking their products out of direct competition with similar products sold through customary retail outlets.

In food products, for example confectionery, the need for freshness of product may be a major reason for selling direct to consumers. Other producers of food products, including meat packers, fisheries, fruit growers, cheese manufacturers, and others, have also utilized this appeal, together with uniqueness and breadth of line, in order to sell direct.

Manufacturers of industrial goods are much more likely to sell direct to users, and for different reasons. Frequently, the services needed by the customer, both in connection with the sale and after the sale, are such that middlemen are not qualified to give them. These include analysis of the customer's needs, product design and adaptation, installation, postsale servicing and repair, and training of customer personnel in operating and servicing. Industrial sales are often large in volume and irregular in occurrence. Negotiations may involve many persons and extend over a long period of time. Although agents may be equipped to handle transactions of this complexity, distributors rarely are. Consequently, the manufacturer may have no real choice but to handle the distribution himself.

The combination of cost and service considerations, which may call for the direct sale of industrial goods, seldom prevails in consumers' goods. The latter are generally distributed much more efficiently through middlemen, at least when compared with the use of direct-to-consumer sales organizations.

Direct Sale to Retailers

Consumer-goods manufacturers may sell directly to retailers but ordinarily do so only when the number of retail outlets involved is limited. These limited numbers arise from two sets of circumstances: (1) where retailers are very large, especially when they are in the large-scale category, which includes chains, department stores, mail-order houses, and cooperatives, and (2) when the manufacturer follows a policy of limited distribution.

Direct contact with large-scale retailers is usually feasible because the retailer buys in large quantities (although this is not true of all lines sold in department stores) and may desire special packing and labeling and other services. Frequently, the retailer obtains promotional allowances; and manufacturer and retailer may undertake joint promotions. When distribution is handled by a limited number of stores, the manufacturer tends to work closely with them and may require some minimum level of performance to justify the franchise. Lacking direct contact with retailers, the manufacturer may find a limited distribution system unsatisfactory, although some firms do turn this responsibility over to distributors.

For some convenience-type products, where merchandising at the retail level is important, such as grocery, drug, and tobacco products, the manufacturer may sell through wholesalers but still have missionary salesmen call on retailers. These salesmen may write orders, which are turned over to wholesalers designated by the retailer, but their primary function is to secure retailer support for the line in the form of product display, point-of-sale advertising, and local advertising. Missionary salesmen may or may not call on all stores, but they will devote their major attention to the larger stores.

Whenever the manufacturer displaces or augments the wholesaler, there is a need to provide the sales and warehouse facilities formerly supplied by the wholesaler, or to supplement them. The result is the creation of manufacturers' wholesale branches. As indicated in Chapter 2, these facilities have been expanding since World War II. Actually, manufacturers' field facilities can take several forms. Some are sales offices only. Some are warehouse facilities only. Many are a combination of the two. Lacking their own field warehouses, food processors, tobacco-products manufacturers, and others may utilize public warehouses.

General versus Limited Distribution

Policies dealing with the level of market contact or depth of channel penetration and with the scope of distribution are intertwined. A manufacturer of convenience-type consumer goods cannot sell directly to the average retailer unless the line is very broad or the typical order is quite large. Market conditions for a product must be such as to make selective distribution feasible. Once the manufacturer is assured that he can get adequate market coverage under this policy, he is in a position to implement it.

Usually, it is not feasible to distribute convenience goods this way. Shopping-type and specialty consumer goods and industrial goods, however, are commonly distributed in this manner. In essence, a policy of selective distribution envisages that only that number of wholesalers and/or retailers is used which is required to give the desired market penetration and permit the manufacturer to reach his market objectives. Sometimes, market objectives can be attained with a policy of exclusive distribution—one outlet in a given market area. In other cases, more than one outlet is needed, and it thereby becomes necessary to determine the proper number of outlets for each area.

There are several reasons why a manufacturer may want to establish a policy of selective distribution among wholesalers, retailers, or both. He deals with a limited number of high-caliber firms. Each can be expected to carry a full line of the manufacturer's products, perform the necessary sales and postsale services, support the manufacturer's promotional programs at the local level, furnish useful market data, and maintain prices when the manufacturer desires that this be done.

The manufacturer can work intensively with the selected outlets and give various types of management and promotional assistance. The working time of the field sales organization can be more profitably used. Customers buy in comparatively large quantities; and credit problems are virtually nil.

The middleman benefits from the manufacturer's support and guidance, although this aid is of greatest value to the smaller, specialty-type store. If the middleman has exlusive rights, the market is his to develop. If others in his area also have the line, he should be able, with proper effort, to get his "share" of sales, unless the manufacturer has oversaturated the market.

There are some dangers in a policy of selective distribution. The manufacturer must be certain that he has a sufficient number of middlemen to cover the market and to secure the desired market penetration. At the wholesale level, selective distribution can be used by most manufacturers of industrial goods and by manufacturers of specialty and shopping-type consumer goods. Some manufacturers of convenience goods, for example drugs, have used a wholesale selective distribution policy successfully.

Actually, at the wholesale level, many manufacturers, and wholesalers as well, would benefit by wider use of selective distribution. By carrying several parallel lines, wholesalers increase their costs and dilute their efforts. Wholesalers may not want to take the risk of reducing the number of competing lines, however, and manufacturers may be hesitant to reduce the number of outlets for fear of loss of sales. More experimentation is needed by both manufacturers and wholesalers in this area to determine the relationships among costs, services, and sales, as manufacturers reduce the number of wholesale outlets and wholesalers reduce the number of parallel lines carried.

At retail, selective distribution is probably effective for most specialty lines and shopping lines, but it is not satisfactory for convenience goods which, by definition, must be available at many locations within easy reach of consumers.

Under a policy of selective distribution, the manufacturer needs at least one outlet, whether wholesale or retail, in each major trading center. With the growth of the market, additional retailers may be selected in surburban areas and secondary trading centers. As new markets are entered, the franchise may be given to only one middleman, but this opens the way to later problems as the sales potential rises and the original middlemen cannot obtain the necessary market penetration. When this point is reached, one or more new outlets must be added, perhaps at the risk of injuring relations with the original outlet. This problem may be forestalled by using exclusive outlets only in centers where the sales potential in the foreseeable future can be handled by one outlet.

Selective distribution must rest on careful market analysis and on a clearly established set of criteria for the types of outlets to be included in the system. Such criteria would be related to size of the distributor/ retailer business, financial responsibility, lines carried, quality of management and drive, reputation in the market, and willingness to cooperate with the manufacturer. Ideally, the distributive system should be expanded to the point where it is attaining the manufacturer's objectives, at which time the system may become comparatively stable.

In Figure 3 additional outlets are added as sales in the market start to level off. These additions are carried to the point where the increase

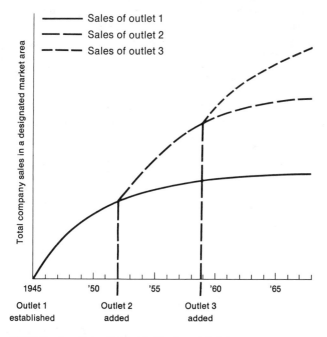

Figure 3 Area Sales Related to Number of Outlets

in sales is not sufficient to attract and hold new outlets, or where the activities of entrants cut too heavily into the sales which the established outlets would otherwise secure.

Dual Distribution

Dual distribution occurs when a company sells the same product line through parallel channels. The term also includes selling two brands of like products—either two manufacturer brands or a manufacturer brand and a distributor brand—through different channels.[1] For example, a manufacturer may sell the same product to wholesalers and also direct to retailers in the wholesaler's trading area; or he may sell to retailers and also operate a retail store in the same market. He may sell raw materials to another manufacturer and also produce comparable finished goods which are sold in competition with his raw-material customers.

A policy of dual distribution is adopted for varying reasons. It may be a device for reaching somewhat different market segments, as where a manufacturer produces identical or very similar products under two brands. Tire manufacturers, for example, have engaged in this practice. A firm may want to make direct contact with the market and so decide to open a few retail outlets; or it may believe it can serve some of its customers better than wholesalers (especially larger customers) and so sell directly to them.

The petroleum industry is a major example of the use of dual distribution. Gasoline is sold under both refiner brands and the brands of independent distributors. As can be seen in Figure 4,

> . . . refiners supply jobbers and also perform the wholesale function on an integrated basis. Refiners supply service stations and also operate service stations; in addition, they also act as landlord of the leased premises of many stations that are supplied by them. Jobbers, too, are often dual distributors acting as suppliers to some stations while operating others which they lease or own.[2]

Those affected by dual distribution, especially competing independent middlemen, have a number of criticisms concerning the practice. One relates to the price squeeze which results when a manufacturer, in his

[1] L. E. Preston, and S. E. Schramm, Jr., "Dual Distribution and Its Impact on Marketing Organization," *California Management Review* (Winter, 1965).

[2] *The Impact upon Small Business of Dual Distribution and Related Vertical Integration,* a report of Subcommittee No. 4 on Distribution Problems to the Select Committee on Small Business, H.R., 88th Cong. 1964, p. 80.

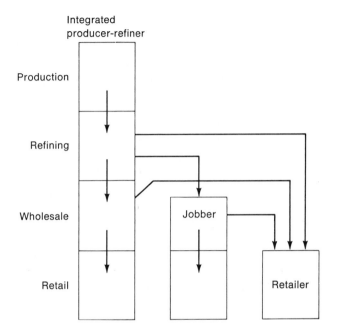

Figure 4 Dual Distribution in Gasoline Marketing

SOURCE: *The Impact upon Small Business of Dual Distribution and Related Vertical Integration,* a reprot of Subcommittee No. 4 on Distribution Problems to the Select Committee on Small Business, U.S. House of Representatives, 88th Congress, 1964, p. 81.

role of supplier, charges a relatively high price, while simultaneously selling at a comparatively low price in his role of seller-competitor. This may occur particularly when sales are made directly to large-scale retailers at prices below those charged competing wholesalers. Unless satisfactory alternative sources of supply are available, the independent wholesaler and his customers may be put at a competitive disadvantage.

In times of merchandise shortages, manufacturers may not supply independent middlemen in order to service their own competing establishments. In other cases, a manufacturer may preempt sales to large customers and leave the wholesaler only the smaller customers. Where a manufacturer opens his own outlets in areas previously served by franchised middlemen, the existing franchises may be canceled. Finally, under conditions where a manufacturer is attempting to penetrate a market with his own distributive facilities, the outlets may be subsidized by the parent organization for varying periods of time.

Because of the threat which dual distribution appears to pose to independent middlemen, a subcommittee of the Select Committee on Small Business of the United States House of Representatives held extensive hearings on the subject in 1963. In the course of the hearings, more than forty industries were examined in order to learn the impact of dual distribution practices and to determine whether special legislation is necessary. The Committee concluded that dual distribution in itself is not harmful to competition but that competition may be endangered when this practice is used for predatory purposes through the exercise of a firm's market power.

The Committee believed that prohibitions against integration and dual distribution would be unwise, but it did recommend that a study of the present antitrust laws be undertaken in terms of their effect on competition, economic growth, integration, and economic concentration. Specifically, it was suggested that a study committee consider whether firms which compete with their own customers should be required to maintain differentials between prices charged as supplier and prices charged as competitor.[3]

In a dynamic marketing structure such as ours, where attempts are being made constantly to improve distribution efficiency, an innovation such as dual distribution cannot be condemned per se. If it results primarily from market power based on some form of monopolistic position, and if the long-range goal is higher prices rather than greater distributive efficiency, then appropriate legislative action may be in the best interests of the economy. In the author's opinion, Congress has wisely deferred action on this issue until more evidence is at hand.

Reciprocity

In the industrial field, it is generally considered to be "good business" to patronize one's customers when their products, services, and prices are the same as those offered by other sources. The same practice is commonly followed by business firms and professional people within a community. The practice of recriprocity, however, frequently goes beyond this rather general, voluntary approach, and it may become a matter of company policy to actually formalize buying-selling relationships

[3] *Ibid.,* pp. 107–108.

with suppliers. When this occurs, either sales or purchasing representatives of a company will approach a supplier who is in a position to use the company's products and point out that since the company is purchasing a given volume from the supplier, the company would like to sell certain of *its* products to the supplier.

The procedures used to bring about reciprocal buying and selling, the amount of pressure applied by the stronger of the two firms, and the formality and degree of "balancing" of trade will vary widely, but the implications of the transaction are the same. The supplier is expected to buy at least a fair share of his needs of a particular product line from the customer firm.

It is difficult to know how extensive recriprocal buying and selling relationships are among industrial firms, since the subject has never been thoroughly studied; but the practice is believed to be quite common.

> It is apparently true that to a greater or less degree reciprocity is found in nearly every type of manufacturing business as well as in banking institutions and insurance, public utility, transportation, and construction companies. It is among manufacturers of industrial goods, however, that the practice is most common. It appears to be particularly prominent among manufacturers of machinery and other iron and steel products, electrical supplies, paper and printing, chemicals (including paints) and nonferrous metals, petroleum, and rubber.[4]

Reciprocity is probably used most often "in mature industries, where the stream of product innovation has long since dried up, where the products made by competing concerns are undifferentiated, and where prices are identical to the penny."[5] Industrial service organizations are particularly vulnerable to customer pressure. Railroads are pressured by their customers, and truckers of petroleum products are expected to buy their fuel from their customers. Even newspapers may be approached by major advertisers with the request that the paper consider making certain purchases from them.

Some reciprocity arrangements take a triangular form, as indicated below. The first example is drawn from the comments of the purchasing officer of a railroad-car manufacturer.

---

[4] W. B. England, *Procurement: Principles and Cases,* 4th ed., Richard D. Irwin, Inc., Homewood, Ill., 1962, p. 486.
[5] E. Raymond Corey, *Industrial Marketing,* Prentice-Hall, Inc., Englewood Cliffs, N.J., 1962, p. 464.

We manufacture only freight equipment, such as box cars, gondola cars, flat cars, and hopper cars for the various railroads which may be good enough to place their orders with us.

During the last several years, due to the reciprocal turn of mind of both seller and buyer, almost all the material used in car construction has been allocated by the railroad for which the cars were being constructed. The real function of buying has been eliminated, and all competition has been voided as far as our own company is concerned. In one instance we received an order for 500 hopper cars, involving 5,600 tons of steel, and were requested by the railroad to split this between seven different steel producers, ranging from 2 per cent as the lowest amount to 45 per cent as the highest.[6]

. . . . .

A manufacturer of sheet metal sells his product to a manufacturer of oil drums. The sheet metal manufacturer having no use for the drums buys its oil from a customer of the drum manufacturer. Again, a construction company is often under pressure from the owner of the proposed building to buy from a particular material supplier because that supplier happens to be a purchaser of the owner's product or a stockholder. The construction company may also feel pressure from the engineer or architect and at the same time want to satisfy other owners who have been clients in the past or may become so in the future.[7]

Reciprocity arrangements may be attractive to a sales department as a device to increase volume, particularly when a firm is at some competitive disadvantage. However, such arrangements place restrictions on the purchasing department which may not be in the firm's best interests.

There may be occasions when it is acceptable to compromise to some degree on purchases, if a clear advantage to sales can be shown. Whenever formal reciprocity is undertaken, however, the purchasing department should keep adequate records of its impact on purchases and other facets of the company's operations.

Reciprocity agreements should be worked out, preferably by a special unit such as a "customer" or "trade-relations" department, under the direction of top management and within a policy framework based on an appraisal of overall company gains and losses from this practice.[8] The appraisal should include an analysis of prospective sales to the firm

[6] England, *op. cit.*, p. 486.

[7] *Ibid.*, p. 487.

[8] Henry G. Hodges, *Procurement,* Harper & Row, Publishers, Incorporated, New York, 1961, pp. 257–260. The Federal government is becoming increasingly interested in reciprocity arrangements as possible violations of the antitrust laws. This subject is discussed in Chapter 4.

in question and the suitability of the supplier's offering (product, service, and price) in terms of the company's real needs.

If purchase requirements are shifting or seem likely to shift, the establishment of a reciprocal arrangement may quickly become a source of embarrassment when the company can no longer fulfill its side of the bargain. When this occurs, the sales department may lose a customer which it might have had without reciprocity if the company had been selling on the basis of goods and services rather than reciprocity.

Reciprocity, therefore, is a policy to be adopted with caution. Otherwise, it may boomerang when market conditions change. Sometimes, firms are forced into it because competitors are bringing pressure on common suppliers. When a company is caught in this situation, it may find it necessary to institute similar arrangements, albeit reluctantly, in order to protect its market position. On balance, "formal" reciprocity is a policy of dubious economic merit. It is a kind of lock-step operation in which the firms involved lose flexibility and freedom of movement in a competitive market.

Wholesaler Distribution Policies

Wholesale establishments find it necessary to identify the market segment they expect to serve and the types of customers to whom they will sell. To some extent, this decision is made when the wholesaler's "line" is decided upon, but market planning procedure properly starts with the market. With the needs of prospective customers in mind, merchandise stocks are then assembled. A wholesale distributor in the electrical field, for example, may choose to sell to a very broad market, such as both hardware stores and industrial establishments, or to a market as specialized as neon-sign manufacturers, electrical repair shops, large electrical contractors, shipyards, and boat works.

Wholesalers also have to decide whether they are going to sell strictly at wholesale or handle a retail business as well. Firms just starting in business may undertake to do both, perhaps because of a thin wholesale market or because they are not sure in which direction they want to go. This is an opportunistic approach. If both portions of the business thrive, they may continue to be operated as separate divisions. Thus, for example, a company may operate a wholesale hardware division and a group of retail hardware stores. This, in effect, is dual distribution as practiced by a wholesaler rather than a manufacturer. Usually, organizations of this type will not operate two parallel divisions with equal success and will tend to close out or sell the less-successful unit.

Once a wholesaler has settled on the market segment he wants to serve, he then devises a marketing strategy (product line, service policy, pricing strategy, and promotional methods) to attain his objectives. Unlike the manufacturer, however, the wholesaler does not adopt a policy of selective distribution within his market segment unless he controls a brand franchise in his trading area. A distributor of a nationally advertised brand of lawnmowers, for example, may be empowered by the manufacturer to select dealers to handle the brand in his area. Other distributors of specialty products may follow a similar procedure. Most wholesalers, however, expect to sell to any firm that fits their customer classifications, and in this sense they engage in general distribution.

Because it is the small retailer or business establishment that depends on wholesalers, many wholesalers are almost automatically faced with the situation of serving a large number of buyers who may purchase often but in small quantities. This creates one of the major dilemmas of wholesale operation. How the wholesaler solves this problem is too complex a subject to discuss in detail here. One step is to prune his lines, particularly parallel lines, in order to increase stock turnover. In effect, this becomes a process of selective buying. Another is to match services to customer profitability by such devices as quantity discounts, reduced sales calls and increased use of mail and telephone orders, service charges, encouragement of cash-and-carry business, etc. To make these decisions, wholesalers need a good cost accounting system, something which relatively few wholesalers have.

Voluntary Chains

In order to strengthen their competitive position, full-service merchant wholesalers in some consumers-goods lines, notably groceries, hardware, and automotive products, have sponsored voluntary chains. The early growth of these chains paralleled the expansion of centrally owned chains following World War I, but the growth has continued into the post-World War II period.

In the establishment of these chains, wholesalers, in effect, create a special group of customers who, by agreeing to certain forms and standards of operation, are thereby entitled to a range of services over and beyond those supplied other customers of the wholesaler. The voluntary group is based on the sound economic assumption that if retailers become better managers, and if they cooperate as a group in order to secure some of the economies of larger-scale operations, all components of the enterprise will be more likely to thrive, particularly against the competition of centrally owned chains.

This wholesale policy, therefore, rests on the economic base of strengthening the wholesale-retail channel and, in some cases, on the pressing need to take this step for survival. In the hardware and automotive-products fields, some of the voluntary organizations sprang full blown in the sense that they served only members of their own group from the beginning. This was true, as well, of the leading voluntary chain in the variety-store field, Ben Franklin stores. In groceries, most voluntaries began by establishing a core of special-service retailers within the customer group. These were usually well-operated stores in key locations. Some wholesalers established more than one such group.

Wholesalers often continued to sell to nonaffiliated retailers, but as voluntary organizations grew in strength, many discontinued sales to nonaffiliates. In some of the most successful voluntary organizations, for example Super Valu stores, headquartered in Minneapolis, even the name of the original wholesale firm was dropped, and the organization assumed the name of the retail group.

The economic strength of the voluntary chain lies in presenting to the public the image of a group of stores, standardized in appearance and general operations, which carry dependable merchandise in adequate variety and at reasonable prices. The stores are well located, pleasant, usually convenient to shop in, and fairly well standardized in layout and merchandise selection. They benefit from centrally planned promotional programs which feature weekly offerings, special sales, and, sometimes, private brands. The price appeal is important, and price-leader advertising is common.

The central voluntary-chain organization performs many services for retail members, starting with help in the selection of a location, planning store design, layout, and merchandise inventories, and even, at times, helping with the financing of the new venture. Actually, some organizations go further than this. They watch for good locational opportunities, start a store themselves, and then turn it over to an independent operator as soon as one can be found.

As a service to stores, the central organization supervises the general management of stores and stands ready to be of assistance when operating difficulties arise. Fieldmen work with store operators, and head-quarter's specialists develop promotional programs, even to the point of preparing tax returns.

For this assistance, the retailer pays a fee which is related to the volume of his business. In order to hold down costs, however, the retailer may have to forego certain other services which historically have been supplied by wholesalers. The most significant of these are personal selling, unlimited delivery service, and credit. A standardized order form to be submitted by mail, on an established schedule, usually replaces the salesman. Deliveries, likewise, are scheduled, often no more than once a week; and store personnel may be expected to help with the unloading. Shipments are virtually on a cash basis. Some organizations require a signed blank check be submitted with the order. Others allow up to a week for payment; but the old thirty-day credit line has been abandoned.

It is expected, of course, that the retailer will purchase virtually all of his merchandise from the wholesaler, although the written contract will not be that specific. Consequently, the wholesaler has a known and dependable market and a stable sales base for purchases and the development of promotional plans. The voluntary chain represents vertical channel cooperation in its most effective form. Properly operated, it benefits all parties and presents an excellent opportunity for entrepreneurs to enter the retail business. Furthermore, voluntary chains—and to some extent, retailer cooperatives also—have served to contain the growth of centrally owned chains, particularly in groceries, as shown in Figure 5. The result is a better-balanced marketing structure than would have prevailed if chains had been able to sweep the field; and this is to the consumer's advantage.

Wholesale Trading Areas

Unlike manufacturers, wholesalers ordinarily do not extend their geographical coverage over anything approaching the national market. There are a few so-called "national" wholesalers of a highly specialized type; but most wholesalers serve a market which may range from a section of a city, at one extreme, to an area which might best be described as regional.

The primary factor responsible for the limited geographical coverage of wholesalers is logistics. Since manufacturers make their products available through wholesalers in various market centers, wholesalers, in

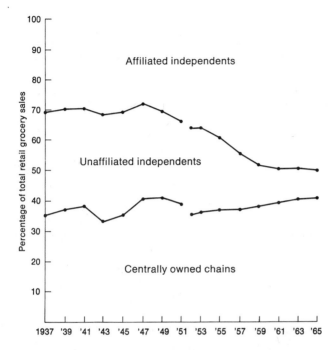

Figure 5 Share of Retail Grocery Sales Taken by Independents and Chains

Note: Through 1951, chains were considered to be firms operating four or more stores. After 1951, the definition of chains was changed to include organizations which had eleven or more stores.

SOURCE: *33rd Annual Report of the Grocery Industry,* Progressive Grocer, New York, April, 1966, p. 155.

turn, can sell only in an area in which they have a cost advantage. The wholesaler is competing in every direction against wholesalers in other centers. The result is a pattern of trading areas in which boundaries are determined largely by transportation costs.

For the guidance of manufacturers and wholesalers, several product maps have been published showing typical coverage of wholesalers located in the principal wholesale trading centers for those products.[9]

Trading areas vary considerably by type of product. Products with a very wide retail distribution base, particularly food and tobacco prod-

[9] For a listing of available trading area maps see Louis D. Volpp, *Statistics and Maps for National Market Analysis, Small Business Bibliography No. 12,* Small Business Administration, Washington, April, 1965.

ucts, have a decentralized wholesale structure and, consequently, comparatively small trading areas. Hardware and dry-goods wholesalers, however, tend to be found only in major cities, and so their trading areas are relatively large.

The specific market covered by a particular wholesaler may or may not correspond with the typical trading area. Actual market coverage is the resultant of the wholesaler's marketing policies and strategy. His basic geographical distribution policy may be one of extensive versus relatively intensive distribution. Under the former, the wholesaler may reach out as far as he can. He may penetrate the natural trading area of another wholesale center by absorbing freight or by selling specialty-type products, perhaps his own brands. He may not travel salesmen at the periphery of the market but rather cultivate this business by mail or telephone. Sometimes, if a wholesaler is larger than his competitors in other centers, the breadth of his line may permit him to sell in their markets. Through these devices, a firm may sell successfully beyond its "normal" trading area. However, such a wholesaler is always under strong pressure from firms which are more economically located with respect to the fringe markets he is trying to reach. He needs to be sure of his strategy, to be aware of alternative uses of his resources, and to have access to a good cost system. Firms which choose to incur the risks of extensive distribution may protect themselves by establishing branches at strategic points. This step enables them to serve a market which can be economically handled from the branch location. Because it is the most satisfactory way of penetrating distant markets, the establishment of branches by wholesalers is a rather common practice.

A policy of intensive distribution within the limits of the normal trading area is easier for a firm to support. Here, maximum effort is applied within the area in which the firm has a basic cost advantage.

As wholesalers extend their geographical markets, they move in the direction of least resistance. They tend to encroach on the markets of secondary centers rather than on those of competing primary centers. Also, they tend to expand in directions which permit them to benefit from the original merchandise movements from supply centers. For example, hardware has been manufactured primarily in the area east of the Mississippi River. Wholesalers to the west, therefore, push their shipments farther west rather than attempt to sell against the primary, westward merchandise flow.

This situation is illustrated in Figure 6. Minneapolis wholesalers find

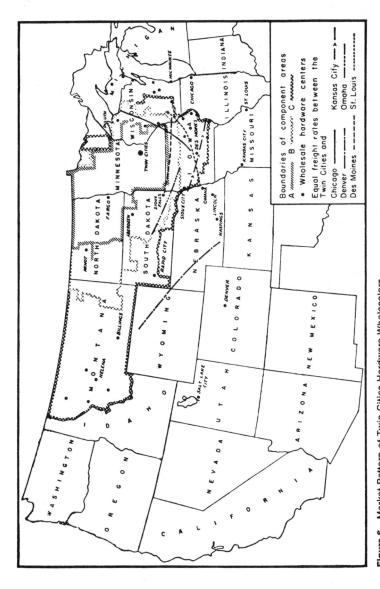

Figure 6 Market Pattern of Twin Cities Hardware Wholesalers

SOURCE: Edwin H. Lewis, *Wholesaling in the Twin Cities*, Studies in Economics and Business, The University of Minnesota Press, Minneapolis, 1952, p 39.

it very difficult to penetrate very far to the east against wholesalers located in Chicago and Milwaukee. It is much more profitable to extend shipments to the west. This example also illustrates the "layered" composition of wholesale markets.[10] The intensity of market coverage normally decreases as wholesalers get farther from the wholesale center. But the thinning effect does not occur equally in all directions. The market terminates rather abruptly as major competing wholesale centers are approached and tapers off gradually in areas of less competition. A similar market pattern was found among Philadelphia wholesalers also studied by the author.[11]

Wholesale-Retail Buying Policies

As purchasers of goods intended for resale, merchant middlemen, in effect, serve as purchasing agents for their customers. Their function is to assemble an assortment of merchandise which will meet the collective needs of their clientele. The lines carried are determined partly by customer requests and partly by the effectiveness of suppliers' promotional activities directed to them and to their markets. Wholesale and retail buying staffs, in almost all lines, are faced with a flood of new merchandise: new products and brands and proliferations of established brands. Buying, therefore, becomes an increasingly complex process of selection.

Presumably, the middleman has a free hand in deciding which lines he will carry, but, in fact, this is not altogether the case. Manufacturers of branded consumer products have found that they can go directly to the user through advertising and promotional media, which frequently, for convenience products, include the use of coupons and samples. When the consumer arrives at a store to redeem a coupon or to replace a sample with a regular package, a chain-ordering procedure is initiated

[10] Edwin H. Lewis, *Wholesaling in the Twin Cities,* Studies in Economics and Business, The University of Minnesota Press, Minneapolis, 1952.

About two-thirds of the sales of Twin Cities hardware wholesalers were made outside the Twin Cities. Of these sales, approximately 70 percent were attributed to area A, 25 percent to area B, and 10 percent to area C. To define the component market areas, wholesalers' sales were totaled by county, and counties were then ranked according to the ratio of wholesalers' sales to retail hardware sales. Area A counties had the highest ratios, area C counties, the lowest.

[11] Edwin H. Lewis, "Wholesale Market Patterns," *Journal of Marketing* (January, 1948).

which it is difficult for retailers and wholesalers to oppose. The manufacturer has "presold" the product and developed a demand which "pulls" the product through the channel of distribution. This may not always work for small, little-known companies, but it is a procedure which the giants in packaged-food products, toilet goods, and household products have been using with great success.

At the retail level, and this is particularly true of supermarkets, the store operator cannot stock every brand of coffee, or cake mix, or soap products offered to him. Supermarket shelves grow steadily longer, but the retailer must continue to be very selective in his choice of lines. The ideal size of a supermarket's selling area (in the view of store operators) was considered to be 8,500 square feet in 1949 and 13,400 square feet in 1965.[12] In 1946, supermarkets carried some three thousand items, on the average. By 1965, this had more than doubled, to seven thousand items.[13] Even with this growth, supermarkets can stock only a fraction of the items available to them.

Within limits, a similar situation exists among other retailers. Manufacturers strive for acceptance among middlemen; and the first task in marketing a new consumer product is to get it into an adequate number of stores—i.e., to get satisfactory "distribution"—and also to get as many package "facings" as possible in each store.

Merchandise decisions are made internally by such large-scale retailers as department stores, chain stores, and mail-order houses. The decisions of small retailers may be governed to a considerable degree by the lines available from their wholesalers. Small retailers may have a choice of several wholesale sources when they are located either within a metropolitan area or at a point served by wholesalers in two or more trade centers. As wholesalers adopt a policy of market expansion, retailers may have a greater number of sources available. But where cost studies dictate a reduction in wholesale market areas, retailers are more restricted in their supply sources. Staples are purchased from wholesalers close at hand. Specialties may be purchased at a greater distance, as may some basic lines when the more distant wholesaler offers lower delivered prices.

Wholesalers of industrial products frequently serve very specialized

[12] *The Supermarket Industry Speaks, 1965,* Super Market Institute, Chicago, 1965.
[13] *33rd Annual Report of the Grocery Industry,* Progressive Grocer, New York, April, 1966, p. 56.

markets, and their objective typically is to carry complete stocks of products needed in these markets. Wholesalers which serve broad industrial markets, however, often have much the same selection problems as wholesalers of consumer goods.

Retail Buying Organizations

Outside buying organizations have been used extensively by department stores and specialty stores. These are of several types: (1) independent buying offices that are paid a fee, generally based on sales volume, by client stores; (2) store-owned or cooperative buying organizations owned by the stores, such as Associated Merchandising Corporation (AMC); (3) chain-owned offices maintained by a chain of stores (e.g., Allied Purchasing Corp., Associated Dry Goods Corp., and May Department Stores); (4) privately owned offices maintained by large stores such as Marshall Field and Neiman-Marcus; and (5) millinery syndicates and similar organizations operating leased departments.[14]

These buying organizations are centered in New York, but they may also maintain buying offices in such market centers as Chicago, Los Angeles, San Francisco, and Miami.

Central buying offices supplement the activities of store buyers. They assist the store buyer on his buying trips and also handle subsequent orders placed in the market. Group buying organizations, such as types (2) and (3) above, usually represent only one store in a city. They may purchase basic lines in large quantity, often under private label. The stores in the group may exchange operating information and undertake joint promotions.

Other retailers, particularly drugstores and grocers, have formed buying groups or clubs which purchase staples in larger quantities than could the stores acting alone. Frequently, these groups are sporadic and informal in their operations. However, some of them have grown into retailer cooperatives which maintain permanent, centralized buying staffs and warehouses. Their emphasis is primarily on low prices; and though store members usually have a common identification, there is little attempt to extend to them management services of the type found in voluntary chains.

---

[14] "New York Buying Offices," *Sales Management* (Sept. 2, 1960), pp. 39ff.

Some retailer cooperatives in Eastern cities were established before the turn of the century. They have been particularly important in drugs, groceries, and hardware; and some of the leaders have been among the strongest and best-entrenched retail organizations in their areas.

Distributor Brands

As large-scale retailers, and occasionally wholesalers, establish themselves in their market and develop a favorable public image, they may decide to take advantage of this image by selling their own brands. This gives rise to the "private" or "distributor" brand. Such brands are widely used by mail-order houses, department stores and store buying groups, centrally owned chains, voluntary chains, retailer cooperatives, consumer cooperatives, and merchant wholesalers. They are applied to a very wide range of consumer goods but are particularly important in food products, toilet goods, apparel, hardware, paint, and automotive supplies.

Most private branders do not manufacture. Rather, they have the goods produced, either by companies which also have their own brands or by firms which specialize in the manufacture of distributor brands in accordance with the buyer's specifications. The private brander negotiates the transaction with the supplier and settles matters of product design, quantities desired, shipping schedules, and price. Shipments are made either to warehouses maintained by the buyer or directly to stores.

There are several reasons why middlemen move into private-brand business. This is one way of offering customers a distinctive line of merchandise not available anywhere else. It is thus a device for building customer loyalty. Such brands carry a wider gross margin than comparable manufacturer brands, and even though the middleman must bear all the selling costs, the contribution to profits is likely to be greater than for manufacturers' brands. The favorable margin also permits management to lower prices and thus attaches to its brands a strong promotional feature. Although distributor brands may be of a quality superior to manufacturers' advertised brands, and may be sold at a higher price, the more common practice is to give consumers the impression that they are buying comparable products at a lower price.

The quality of distributor brands, however, must be of a level acceptable to the consumer; and careful attention must be given to quality and design features and to quality control. Private brands have the potential for injuring a store's image as well as enhancing it.

One effect of distributor brands is to broaden the range of competition. Consumers can make comparisons among manufacturers' brands and distributor brands taken together. The consumer thus has a wider range of choice when considering such factors as product performance, price, and "prestige value" of the brand. The basic formula of good quality at a relatively low price has been very successful for many private branders, and their brands have frequently captured a substantial share of the market.

Policies of Industrial Buyers

By and large, industrial purchases are handled by professionals who understand product performance, are able to seek out the most satisfactory sources of supply in relation to company needs, and can evaluate price, service, and the other factors which affect industrial sales. Purchases of large equipment are generally made direct from the manufacturer. Users of large quantities of industrial supplies and miscellaneous equipment may also buy direct. Items used by smaller companies usually will be purchased from one of several types of industrial distributors.

As indicated in an earlier section, reciprocity arrangements may influence the choice of supplier. Likewise, when a firm is tied to others through the corporate financial structure, sources of supply may again be predetermined.

Large companies tend to use a "preferred-supplier" list. Suppliers may be rated on certain criteria, and purchases will be made from a few firms at the top of the list in some predetermined manner. Most companies want at least two sources of supply for each item, in order to be sure of filling their needs and to maintain some competition among suppliers. Once a company becomes a "preferred source," it may expect regular orders, provided working relationships between buyer and seller continue to be satisfactory. Such preferred lists of suppliers should be reviewed and revised annually, at least.

At times, firms may not have adequate sources of supply readily available. When this occurs, they may establish new sources, and in the process may find it necessary to give management and financial assistance to the new supplier. Also, the sponsoring firm will probably agree to take all, or at least a substantial part, of the firm's output. The mail-order houses, automobile manufacturers, and food canners are types of businesses which have encouraged new suppliers by these devices.

Responsibility for buying items needed in the normal course of operations will usually rest in the purchasing department. Major machinery and equipment purchases, however, will typically involve several top company executives, and the final arrangements may be negotiated by the chief executive.

Several factors enter into an industrial purchase decision. These include general product quality, durability, dependability, price, economy of operation, maintenance requirements, attendant labor costs, and safety. In addition to evaluating specific products, the industrial buyer finds it necessary to evaluate the vendor, because the satisfaction arising from product use rests on a broader base than product features. Various questions concerning the vendor need to be answered. Does the vendor have the technical know-how needed to adapt his products to customer requirements and to ensure that they will function properly? Does he have adequate plant facilities? Can he be depended upon to meet scheduled deliveries? Is the vendor organization well managed, financially sound, and cooperative in its dealings with customers? Are plant locations favorable in terms of shipping time and transportation costs? It may be difficult to secure answers to all these questions as they pertain to new suppliers, but an attempt should be made to get them.

In multiunit companies, purchasing activities may be centralized or decentralized among the several units. Decentralization, however, is not very satisfactory unless the units require very different products, and even then there are substantial advantages in centralization. Since industrial purchasing should be a professional activity, purchasing standards can be most closely controlled and followed under centralization. Consistent purchasing policies can be followed, better specifications can be established, controlled inspection procedures can be instituted, and continuing research and testing of proposed products and substitutes can be carried out. There are also opportunities for securing lower prices and for cutting purchasing costs. Discounts can be maximized, and an optimum number of suppliers can be established for each product category. These advantages generally outweigh the claims of flexibility and local adaptation made by proponents of decentralization in purchasing.

Buying Policies of the Federal Government

A basic policy of Federal government procurement is to give "all known responsible suppliers" an equal chance to compete for government business.[15] Each agency of the government, both civilian and military, is responsible for its own procurement and may purchase directly from suppliers. Purchases of items in common use, however, are usually consolidated through the General Services Administration (GSA) or the Defense Supply Agency (DSA).

With certain specified exceptions (including some of major importance, such as conditions of national emergency and public exigency), purchases are made under a bidding system. When this is not practical and economical, agencies may negotiate purchases with responsible suppliers.

The Federal Supply Service of GSA procures commonly used items either for stock in GSA warehouses or for direct shipment to user agencies. Nonstock items in general use may be purchased under definite-quantity consolidated purchase contracts or indefinite-quantity term contracts called Federal Supply Schedules. Under these schedules, agencies place orders for their needs direct with the supplier. Stock items are requisitioned by civilian or military agencies.

The Defense Materials Service, also part of GSA, purchases strategic and critical materials for the national stockpile.

Products used by two or more of the military services are frequently purchased by a single department for all military users under the Department of Defense Single Department Procurement program. Thus, the Navy buys coal for the armed services. In other cases, armed-services procurement responsibility lies in one of the several Defense Supply Centers of the Defense Supply Agency. These centers specialize by type of commodity—for example, petroleum products or electronic equipment. Products needed by the armed services and not obtained under either of these programs are ordered directly from suppliers

[15] *Doing Business with the Federal Government*, General Services Administration, 1962.

(specialized military equipment) or secured through the GSA, in the case of products in common use.

Government purchases are made on the basis of GSA or military specifications and must be inspected and approved before payment is authorized.

6

Channel
Decisions

Decisions as to the channels through which goods will be bought and sold are made to some degree by all members in the channel—producer, middleman, and consumer. Producers choose among alternative channel possibilities for the sale of their products. Middlemen determine the market segment and the kinds of customers they want to reach. All parties make use of the available channels to search out goods of the type needed.

Buyers and sellers, consequently, to the extent that alternative channels are available, are faced with the need to make decisions as to the specific channels to be used for sales, or purchases, or both. Such decisions may be quite casual, as when the consumer buys a convenience-type product, or quite complex, as when a manufacturer decides to establish his own wholesale branches or to shift from general to selective distribution.

Channel Decisions as Part of Marketing Mix

Channel decisions, like other decisions concerning the marketing mix, must be consistent with management's marketing goals. These goals may be expressed in terms of sales volume or market share, either for total sales or product-line sales. Management may be primarily interested in developing specific market segments such as particular product uses, customer groups, or geographical markets.

A manufacturer of industrial equipment, for example, who sells to established markets through his own salesmen, may decide to reach new user industries through manufacturers' agents or distributors who specialize in these industries. Similarly, companies which are expanding geographically may want to start with agents in new areas in order to minimize the risks and costs of entering these markets.

Channel decisions must also be consistent with other parts of the marketing mix. A manufacturer of a limited line of convenience items in food or drugs has little prospect of selling direct to the retail trade. As lines are added, he may have a better chance of selling direct. Conversely, as product lines become very broad, as in shoes, it may be difficult to induce retailers to carry the complete line unless they are protected by an exclusive- or limited-distribution franchise.

If the manufacturer wants middlemen to handle the physical distribution function—to maintain complete inventories and make delivery —he will need to sell to full-service wholesalers or large-scale retailers, frequently on a selective-distribution basis.

A promotional policy which requires the active support of retailers, perhaps in the form of cooperative advertising, is difficult to implement if the manufacturer sells primarily through wholesalers. The same would be true in cases where the retailer must furnish special services, such as fitting and installation.

A product which has fluctuating prices, e.g., some food products, could not be distributed satisfactorily under a policy of selective distribution. Instead, such products tend to move through merchant wholesalers on a general-distribution basis.

It may be seen, therefore, that channel decisions are related to the other factors in the marketing mix as these factors are related to one another. To be effective, marketing strategy must be a coordinated strategy. Each element in the mix, of necessity, must support the others. Otherwise, the marketing program will lack direction and drive, and the participants in the program will be working at cross-purposes.

Not only must channel decisions be consistent with other marketing policies; marketing activities inside the company must be compatible with those activities carried out in an environment outside the company:

> . . . a channel of distribution embraces both intracompany organization units and extra-company agents and dealers. Another way to look at it is that a firm's marketing organization consists of (a) one or more organization units within the firm and (b) a system of business units outside the firm, both of which it uses in its marketing work. If a company's marketing program is to be effective, the activities of the inside units and those of the outside units must be closely coordinated so as to make a single, forceful impact on the market. A manager who thinks of the inside organization units in one frame of reference and of the extra-firm units in another is likely to be handicapped in achieving such coordination.[1]

[1] Ralph S. Alexander, and Thomas L. Berg, *Dynamic Management in Marketing,* Richard D. Irwin, Inc., Homewood, Ill., 1965, p. 271.

Allocation of Functions among Units in Channel

To the extent that he has some control over the channel, the manufacturer will decide on the allocation of marketing functions, at least between himself and the first link in the channel. At the one extreme, he may shift most of the responsibilities for marketing to someone else. For example, the textile manufacturer who produces for the garment trades and who operates in a market where style and price are of primary importance may shift the entire selling function to a selling agent. In some instances, the accounts-receivable risk and product planning may be shifted to the agent, as well. Goods are processed on order, and if finished-goods inventories are needed, they are carried by the manufacturer. Since they lack marketing know-how and financial strength, these manufacturers shift virtually the entire marketing responsibility to their agents.

A small manufacturer of a limited line of industrial equipment will frequently decide to turn over most of his selling activity to a group of manufacturers' agents, with each covering a designated market area. He may, however, decide to cover certain key markets through his own salesmen and appoint agents to handle the balance of the business. He has different reasons than those of the textile firm for selling through agents. Since agents carry several allied lines, they can generally sell at lower cost than their principals can. In those markets where the manufacturer can use his own salesmen efficiently, he may choose to do so. Furthermore, the functions of product planning and development, customer financing, and warehousing remain with the manufacturer, and he will often provide backup technical assistance, as well. As sales volume increases and product lines expand, manufacturers may decide to take over the entire sales responsibility and dispense with agents. This, in fact, is one of the risks a manufacturers' agent takes, and he needs to hedge against it by building a balanced group of accounts so that the loss of a single account will not be disastrous.

Manufacturer-Retailer Channel

A local canner may sell his entire output to a food chain or a large wholesaler, perhaps under private label. Selling costs are negligible, shipments are made during the canning season—so there are no processor inventories, and payment is made shortly after receipt of the goods. Virtually all marketing costs are borne by the buyer. He even absorbs the risk of price changes. Since the canner adds little marketing value, his margin above processing costs will tend to be very narrow.

Similarly, a manufacturer of standardized home furnishings, either unbranded or private-branded, may sell virtually all of his output to a mail-order house, a dry-goods chain, or a department store buying group on a sheduled-shipment basis. Again, marketing responsibilities are shifted in large part to the buyer, and the manufacturers' marketing margins are low. In the purchase of any product lacking a brand franchise, where most of the searching costs are borne by the buyer, the buyer's marketing margin will be relatively high and the seller's relatively low.

Manufacturers who sell directly to smaller retailers, whether under a policy of selective distribution or general distribution, must assume the role of channel leader. They must secure adequate distribution in some relation to market potential; encourage retailers to carry satisfactory stocks, both in breadth and depth; make deliveries in quantities acceptable to the retailer; carry the credit risk; furnish various types of management aids; and, frequently, advertise to consumers. The searching costs, physical distribution costs, and financing costs are thus borne largely by the manufacturer.

In this type of situation, the retailer's decisions are limited largely to whether he wishes to carry the line; and where the manufacturer has directed his promotion to the consumer, the retailer may actually not have much choice, if this promotion has stimulated a substantial demand. The retailer also can decide to what extent he wants to cooperate with the manufacturer in supporting the manufacturer's marketing strategy. Depending on their relative positions and the alternatives available to each, the retailer will have some freedom in this respect. To a large degree, however, the manufacturer is the dominant factor in this channel.

In order to sell directly to small retailers, the manufacturer who covers a broad geographical market will often establish stock-carrying sales branches, or if his field sales offices do not carry stocks, he will use public warehouses. In such commodity fields as drugs, dairy products, bakery goods, electrical appliances, industrial machinery, and professional equipment, sales of manufacturers' branches with stocks are considerably greater than sales of branches without stocks.[2]

[2] Bureau of the Census, U.S. Department of Commerce, *Census of Business, Wholesale Trade, United States Summary,* 1963.

Manufacturer-Consumer Channel

A manufacturer who sells direct to the ultimate consumer assumes complete responsibility for the performance of the channel functions. He decides on the method of contact—mail, field sales force, or retail store—and handles the details of physical distribution and financing. Only specialty products sold on a quality or, sometimes, a price appeal can be distributed through this channel. The "product" may include certain services desired by the consumer such as being custom-made. The attractiveness of the product may also be enhanced by offering a wide range of selection.

In the direct sale of industrial goods, the marketing functions are usually shared between manufacturer and user. The searching activity particularly will be shared, and in a given case either party may take the initiative. In such purchases, the buyer may have certain requirements, especially for products purchased as original equipment, which the manufacturer will have to meet. These may pertain to product design, packaging, price, payment terms, deliveries, and special services.

The manufacturer of industrial products is not the channel leader in the sense that he may be for consumer goods. Rather, the manufacturer is likely to accede to the buyer's wishes as long as they are reasonable and the transaction is profitable. The larger the sale, the greater is the bargaining power of the buyer, assuming that alternative sources of supply are available.

Manufacturer-Wholesaler Channel

During the mid-nineteenth century, wholesalers were often more dominant members of the channel than manufacturers. This is less true today, but it may still apply to small manufacturers of shopping or convenience goods. Unless the manufacturer has established his brand through advertising, he may find it difficult to persuade wholesalers to carry the line. This may occur particuarly with respect to new products in competition with others that are well established.

If the manufacturer advertises to the consumer, this may create sufficient leverage that wholesalers will stock the line as they get orders from retailers. Depending on this leverage, manufacturers will attempt to establish terms of sale, sometimes prices, and other sale conditions.

Manufacturers would like to be able to select the wholesalers to carry their products and to expect that these wholesalers will work closely with them in promotional and service activities. But when a manufacturer is in a weak competitive position, this probably will not be possible. As a result of these varying conditions, the balance of power may rest sometimes with the manufacturer, sometimes with the wholesaler. Large wholesalers may have a status equivalent to that of large-scale retailers. They may make the same demands and may even move into private brands. When this occurs, the manufacturer must adapt to the needs of the wholesaler in order to secure distribution.

Wholesaler-Retailer Relations

In dealing with a full-service wholesaler, retailers expect a full range of services—complete stocks, prompt delivery, open-account credit, and some merchandising or technical assistance. For the purchase of products in which freshness is important, a special-service wholesaler, the truck distributor, sells and makes immediate delivery.

The established wholesale services are expensive, however. In some highly competitive fields, particularly groceries, retailers have been willing to absorb some of these services in order to secure lower prices. One of the best examples of this shifting of functions is found in the operations of the cash-and-carry grocery wholesaler. This limited-function wholesaler has appeared in some cities to meet the needs of retailers willing to assume the credit and delivery functions themselves. Some of these establishments are branches of regular, full-service wholesalers.

The operating expenses of the several types of grocery wholesalers reflect these variations in functions performed, as indicated in Table 7.

TABLE 7

Operating Expenses of Grocery Wholesalers (Percent of Sales)

	1963	1958
General-line grocery wholesalers:		
Voluntary groups	6.2⎱	5.3
Retailer cooperatives	4.5⎰	
Other general-line grocers	9.2	8.4
Limited-function wholesalers:		
Cash-and-carry wholesalers	n.a.	6.0
Wagon, truck distributors*	13.0	14.7

*All commodity lines; n.a., not available.
Source: Bureau of the Census, *Census of Business, Wholesale Trade, United States Summary,* 1963.

The costs of truck distributors are high, for example, because they carry limited lines and give store-door service in small quantities.

From the above discussion it is apparent that the status of the manufacturer vis-à-vis the other members in the channel and the status of the other members among themselves changes over time. These changes may occur as the manufacturer moves through his own growth cycle. They occur also as new types of middlemen appear at both the wholesale and retail levels. Finally, they occur as the needs and capacities of consumers change.

Functions are thus being shifted constantly in the vertical channel: more at some times than others (particularly times of economic stress), more in some product lines than others (the grocery field has been particularly dynamic), and more in some areas than others (changes generally occur first in urban areas).

Channels are characterized by a continuous probing and testing. Manufacturers aggressively look for new outlets and new ways to divide up marketing tasks. Buyers—industrial, consumer, and retail—are looking for better "deals." They are constantly searching for new and better (including less-expensive) sources of supply. New purchase opportunities are explored. The performance of channel functions is weighed against the cost, and the available alternatives are being continually studied. The results of such analyses indicate whether integration forward from the manufacturer or backward, particularly from the retailer, would be desirable.

This high degree of flexibility in channel choice and use, and in the mix of functions performed, is one of the strengths of the American economic system. And it is a concept which might well be exported to other countries of the world to their benefit.

Qualitative Channel-decision Factors

Channel decisions for a manufacturer are frequently complex and based on many factors. Most of these factors, including the product line, the nature of the market, the capabilities of the manufacturer, competitive practices, and legal restraints, are qualitative in nature. They must be weighed subjectively, and their impact must be taken into consideration, but their effect is not really measurable. They constitute a checklist of channel determinants which management must recognize.

There are some measurable factors, however, which can help in making channel decisions. These include such performance data as sales, market share, dealer acceptance, consumer awareness and preference, and channel costs. These data enable management to check market attainment against the costs of securing these results.

Taken together, the qualitative and the measureable or quantitative factors form the basis for channel decisions. Using these factors, management may construct a channel-decision model that will contain all the significant variables which underlie a channel decision.

The Product Line

One important set of qualitative factors is related to the product line. Products vary in unit value, in their weight and bulk, in their degree of perishability, and in the extent to which they are standardized. Short channels, involving few if any middlemen, tend to be used when products are high in value (automobiles, pianos) or technical in nature (industrial machinery), when they are heavy or bulky (construction materials), when there is an important element of physical perishability or fashion (fluid milk, women's apparel), and when products are quite distinctive and unique (industrial and professional equipment). These are commodity fields where wholesalers are less likely to be used. When the reverse situations exist, wholesalers are much more likely to be used.

The development stage of a product and the growth stage of the company itself have a bearing on the channels used. If a company starts with a rather limited line of unknown products, it probably will depend heavily on full-service, merchant wholesalers and may also sell through agents rather than attempt to develop its own sales organization. As the line becomes better known and as it broadens in scope, the company probably will experiment with shorter channels. The agent may be displaced, and the company may sell increasingly to retailers.

Characteristics and Requirements of the Market

In addition to product characteristics, the various market factors impinge strongly on channel decisions. These fall into two categories: the nature and geographical distribution of customers, and the needs and requirements of these customers.

The types of customers—ultimate consumer, commercial, industrial, institutional, and governmental—and the segments within these customer groups, such as upper-income families, families with sporting interests, supermarkets, apparel manufacturers, hotels, and police departments, are major determinants of the channels used. Their relative numbers, location, and degree of geographical concentration are additional determinants. Other things being equal, the more highly specialized the market and the more concentrated it is geographically, the shorter the channel will be.

Consumers of all types have specific needs and requirements related to the characteristics of the product or service being offered, the scope of the line and depth of stocks, the type of packaging, and customer services, including repair and parts availability, installation, guarantees, technical aid and consultation, satisfactory terms of sale, acceptable delivery arrangements, and adequate provision for returns and adjustment. Consequently, the source from which the user buys will be governed to a substantial degree by these needs.

The dentist, for example, will purchase his professional needs from a dental supply house or from the branch of a major manufacturer. Restaurants purchase food from wholesalers who specialize in the kinds of products they desire, and obtain their equipment and other operating supplies from restaurant-supply houses. Barbershops purchase from wholesalers who specialize in these supplies. The American marketing structure is highly flexible. As soon as a substantial market segment with special needs can be identified, a supplier will appear to satisfy it.

Not only customer needs but customer buying practices determine the point of purchase. If the housewife plans her weekly needs and shops once a week, she probably will go to a favored supermarket or perhaps patronize more than one in the same area. If she purchases in small quantities in terms of immediate needs, and particularly if she holds a job, she is likely to go to the neighborhood superette or dairy store which is open evenings and Sundays. Consequently, whether orders are large or small, frequent or infrequent, planned or unplanned, and whether purchases must be made at a given time or can be postponed are factors which affect the channels used. The frequent, small purchase is characteristic of convenience goods. The infrequent, postponable purchase is characteristic of shopping and specialty goods.

Companies which produce several lines going to different markets often find it necessary to use multiple marketing channels. This situation is illustrated by Figure 7, which diagrams the several marketing

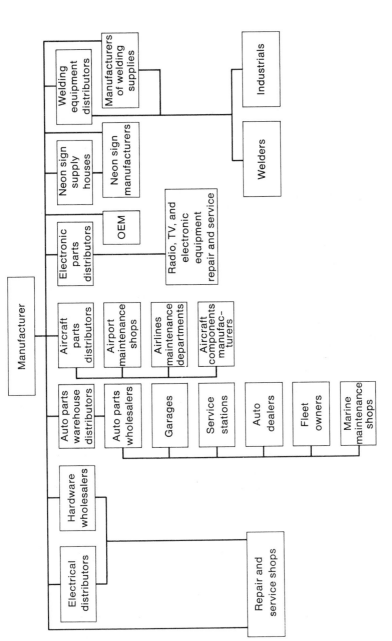

Figure 7 Channels of Distribution of a Manufacturer of Electrical Wire and Cable

SOURCE: Edwin H. Lewis, *Marketing Electrical Apparatus and Supplies*, McGraw-Hill Book Company, New York, 1961, p. 215.

channels used by a manufacturer of specialty electrical wire and cable whose output goes to many different kinds of users.

Capability of the Manufacturer

The marketing strength of the manufacturer is another major qualitative factor in the channel decision. This incorporates marketing management capability and know-how; financial strength and availability of capital for investment in field sales and warehouse facilities, inventories, and customer accounts receivable; and the reputation which the company has established in the market in terms of its products and services. The leading companies in packaged consumer products such as food, soap, and toilet goods have built a tremendous consumer franchise as the result of a growing line of good-quality products, wide distribution, and very aggressive promotion. Although they may continue to use wholesalers where it is more efficient to do so, they also have widespread merchandising contacts with retailers. Their marketing power enables them to shorten the channel, at least for the performance of some retail services.

Conversely, many textile manufacturers, although large producers, have virtually no contact with the market and depend on the know-how and market position of selling agents.

Some merchant middlemen perform rather limited services for the manufacturer, particularly when they handle goods on a general-distribution basis. In other instances, manufacturers depend heavily on middlemen, especially retailers, for promotional support at the local level, for the performance of various customer services, and for feedback of information covering product movement and market conditions. Although wholesalers will be used in both instances, direct contact with retailers will be increasingly important under the latter circumstances.

Competitive Practices

There is a tendency for competitive products to be sold through the same channels, and a similar tendency holds for related noncompetitive products in the same general field. People expect to buy related items at the same source. From time to time, however, some firms break away from established channels and experiment with new outlets. This happened when supermarkets added nonfood lines. In this instance, consumers were willing to buy certain toilet-goods items, dry goods, and household products in conjunction with their food purchases. As a result, supermarkets have become major distributors of toilet goods.[3] A generation ago, toilet goods were purchased primarily in drugstores, although variety stores had entered this field, as had the mail-order houses and some department stores. Now, department stores are expanding their toilet goods and cosmetic departments and, more recently, discount stores in addition to supermarkets have become well established in this field. Meanwhile, the druggist has added other merchandise lines to bolster his sagging share of the rapidly expanding toilet-goods market.

On another front, the retail druggist is losing his near-monopoly of the prescription business. Discount stores and department stores have hired pharmacists and have entered this field. With this development, the competitive position of the drugstore has come full circle. The drugstore was about the first of the so-called single-line stores to add diverse lines: confectionery, soda fountain services, stationery, specialty food products, magazines and periodicals, toys, jewelry, tobacco products—almost anything in the convenience-goods category. Many stores, although classified by the Bureau of the Census as drugstores, have actually been general-merchandise stores. Now, general-merchandise stores have, in turn, invaded the inner domain of the retail druggist.

On balance, while the existing channel practices of competitors need to be noted, and probably met in most cases, manufacturers need to be particularly alert to new channel opportunities. Firms which are willing to experiment with new kinds of outlets in a controlled manner may secure a competitive advantage over rivals, at least temporarily, in the form of wider distribution. However, distribution through new types of outlets may anatagonize existing dealers. This would, therefore, not be a very satisfactory move for manufacturers selling under a limited-distribution policy, unless they were forced to meet the inroads of competitors. Firms selling well-established products under a general-distribution policy have much less to lose. If their products are in substantial demand by consumers, retailers may be expected to carry the line.

[3] Virtually all supermarkets stock "health and beauty aids" and sell about $2 billion annually (*33rd Annual Report of the Grocery Industry,* Progressive Grocer, New York, April, 1966, p. 62).

Suitability of Channels

The rapidity with which new channels evolve is largely dependent on the satisfaction of channel members with existing channels. Manufacturers must see greater opportunities for profit in new channels. Existing middlemen may not be performing in the most desirable way, but satisfactory alternatives may not be available. In time, however, new channels are likely to appear. This occurred with the development of the truck distributor in the grocery field and the rack jobber in the nonfood lines sold to supermarkets.

Since the functions performed by middlemen are elastic and subject to change, wholesalers and retailers can enhance their acceptance by adding new functions or performing existing functions better. Thus, general-line, full-service wholesalers have improved their sales-promotion activities; they cooperate more closely with manufacturers in product introductions and special promotions; and they perform technical services useful to their customers. In the dry-goods field, for example, some have reduced their lines and operate largely on a franchise basis. By improving their services, middlemen reduce the risk that the manufacturer will find more acceptable alternatives.

Legal Restraints on Channel and Customer Selection

There are no Federal laws which indicate the channels of distribution that must be followed in the marketing of goods. On the contrary, Section 2 of the Clayton Act states that:

> Nothing herein contained shall prevent persons engaged in selling goods, wares or merchandise in commerce from selecting their own customers in bona fide transactions and not in restraint of trade.

Thus, a firm may establish criteria concerning the types of customers to whom it will sell, but it must arrive at these criteria independently, not through collusion or conspiracy with other firms. The courts will ordinarily uphold a firm's decision to "refuse to sell" provided the device is not used to create a monopoly.

The problem of customer selection is particularly acute when manufacturers want to engage in selective distribution in order to control resale prices, inventories carried by middlemen, services performed, promotional activities, or other aspects of distribution. With the growth of discount houses in the post World War II period, many manufacturers have struggled to prevent "unauthorized distribution" through these outlets. By watching their "authorized" outlets closely, they can forestall resale of sizable quantities of their lines to discount houses. This requires constant vigilance, however, and even then some overstocks may dribble through the discounter's "back door." Legally, a manufacturer may refuse to sell to discounters, but he may have difficulty closing off completely the pipelines that lead to them (see Chapter 4, pages 75–79).

Although the Federal government has maintained a "hands-off" policy with respect to channel and customer selection, states and local governments have on occasion imposed some restrictions. This has occurred at the state level with respect to liquor and drugs particularly.

Some states specify that liquor for consumption off the premises must be sold through specially licensed establishments, and these establishments may be limited as to number and location. Other states restrict packaged-liquor sales to state-owned stores. Some states, of course, are dry or permit local option, while others exercise virtually no control over off-premises sales.

Under the laws of many states, prescription drugs and, sometimes, proprietary medicines as well may be sold only by stores which employ licensed pharmacists.

Local governments may add to channel restrictions, particularly in relation to the sale of goods at retail, by requiring licenses for the handling and sale of certain food and beverage products. Some communities also control house-to-house sales and canvassing by requiring that direct-selling agencies register or be licensed.

Quantitative Factors in Channel Selection

Although the qualitative factors outlined above all bear on the choice of channels, in the final analysis the deciding factor is which channel provides the greatest profit contribution and the largest return on capital investment. A short channel increases the control which a manufacturer can exercise over distribution, but it is likely to require a heavier investment in inventory, field facilities, sales manpower, and perhaps accounts receivable. The manufacturer needs to consider whether this is the best use of the additional capital compared with alternative uses within the firm.[4]

Under this opportunity-cost concept, manufacturers should absorb channel functions only to the extent that they maximize return on investment in the light of alternative uses for the funds involved. The opportunity-cost approach provides a guide for the vertical integration of marketing functions. In general, the fewer the number of middlemen employed the greater is the financial investment required by the manufacturer.

Similarly, as manufacturers put time and effort into working with middlemen, they are, in effect, making another kind of investment, an investment in customers.[5] It becomes as necessary to judge the return on this type of expenditure as it does to appraise any other part of the marketing mix. Any attempt to determine return on investment in channels of distribution, particularly when investment is defined broadly enough to include expenditures incurred in customer development, assumes that the capital outlay and the costs incurred to create the investment are known. It may be relatively simple to determine the actual capital outlay for a particular channel, but it is usually difficult to calculate the costs incurred in building and strengthening numbers of customers.

What costs should be considered in figuring a company's "investment" in customers? Manufacturer-distributor-dealer relations are built up from many contacts and services, typically over a long period of time. These include the efforts of salesmen and supervisory sales personnel, shipping departments, credit personnel, service-department people, and others. Most of these individuals are engaged in multifunction activities. Furthermore, it is probably difficult to say *which* specific activities serve to strengthen customer contacts.

Profitability of customers (gross margin contribution less marketing costs attributable to them) is almost as difficult to ascertain as return on investment. Even though profit analysis is confined to a definite time period and the *kinds* of cost incurred are known, the proper allocation of these costs may be almost impossible to determine. This problem

---

[4] Eugene W. Lambert, Jr., "Financial Considerations in Choosing a Marketing Channel," *Business Topics,* Michigan State University, East Lansing (Winter, 1966).
[5] Edward C. Bursk, "View Your Customers as Investments," *Harvard Business Review* (May–June, 1966).

springs from the fact that most marketing costs are joint costs, and *any* kind of allocation—whether by product, area, channel, customer group, size of order, etc.—is difficult to make unless direct or escapable costs only are included.

Bursk gets around this problem, in part, by calculating investment in customers in relation to their yield. This procedure may be used when dealing with customer groups. Some of the same problems outlined above are encountered, however, when an attempt is made to assign costs to relatively small customer groups.

> You are the owner, let's say, of a typical wholesale drug company which has $5,000,000 of sales per year on a capital investment (in the usual sense of the word) of $1,500,000. Suppose also that your company has 400 customers, and its gross margin plus cash discounts comes to 15%. Thus you start with 15% of $5,000,000 or $750,000. Now, take off the costs of selling, delivery, a little for postage and telephone and even bad debts— the variable costs associated directly with servicing your customers—which might add up to $350,000. (Consider everything else overhead and profit.) This leaves you with $750,000 minus $350,000 or $400,000—the *annual contribution* that your customers make to your overhead and profit, or the *return on investment* represented by your customers.
>
> You can translate this into investment per average customer (or even better, as will show up when we look at marketing decisions, into investment in particular sizes or kinds of customers). In this case, if your investment criterion is a 10% return (based on other possible uses for money), then your average customer should be worth $10,000 to you— $400,000 divided by 400, or a $1,000 contribution to overhead and profit, in turn divided by 10%. In other words, you have 400 investments, each worth $10,000, for a total of $4,000,000—far more than your investment in conventional physical or financial assets ($1,500,000).[6]

Time Factor in Channel Selection

Channel selection involves both short-run and long-run considerations. It is hoped by all parties concerned that a channel will prove to be effective in sales and efficient in cost in a comparatively short period of time. On occasion, a new channel may be opened when a firm wants to experiment with a new market segment or perhaps close out surplus stocks. Thus, a nonfood manufacturer may initiate sales through supermarkets, or a company may dispose of a surplus through discount

[6] *Ibid.*

stores. These may turn out to be temporary deviations from the firm's regular channels. Sometimes, seasonal merchandise moves through additional or special channels, as when filling stations stock garden supplies in the spring.

Channel innovations of this type are quite fluid, as manufacturers attempt to increase buyer exposure to their line. There is a policy of expediency in these situations, as the manufacturer strives to give his product some of the characteristics of convenience goods. When there is a comparatively short season, manufacturers and/or distributors may literally "flood" the market to facilitate maximum sales, sometimes selling directly to consumers.

Except for distress merchandise and products which are perishable and seasonal, most sellers are concerned with building stable, dependable channels. Manufacturers, and perhaps wholesale middlemen, incur an investment in establishing and strenghtening their outlets. As the parties learn to work together, they become more effective in moving goods and more efficient in doing the tasks assigned. It is sometimes said that the channel and particularly the transactions within the channel become routinized. Routinization may follow negotiation, as when subsequent orders are placed by a mail-order house following negotiation of the original contract, or as industrial buyers continue to purchase raw materials and supplies once the exact nature of the goods and services desired has been agreed upon.[7]

Channel costs will be lowest when stable relations have been created among the parties in a channel and as many functions as possible have been reduced to routine. Whenever transactions must be negotiated, costs rise. Obviously, some channels may never experience the situation in which most functions are performed routinely. This would be the case for industrial equipment and machinery, for example.

Innovation and Channel Selection

The dynamics of the marketplace may, in some industries, result in frequent reappraisal of channels and the introduction of new channels:

The marketing manager who completes a job of organizing or reorganizing his channels cannot heave a sigh of relief and relax in the confi-

[7] For a discussion of negotiated versus routine transactions see Wroe Alderson, *Marketing Behavior and Executive Action*, Richard D. Irwin, Inc., Homewood, Ill., 1955, pp. 295–304.

dence that his channel problems have been solved for a while. For the unit membership in a channel is constantly changing; some forms go out of business or, for reasons of their own, drop out of the channel, and the managerial personnel of an outlet changes with the result that its performance is improved or worsened.

The very nature of the outlets in a trade may change over a period of years, as is exemplified by the growth of the suburban shopping-center store, the supermarket, and the discount house. The manufacturer who delays too long in shifting his channel in response to such changes may find their opportunities closed to him when he finally gets around to capitalizing on them. Managing channels is a constant day-to-day process.[8]

The marketing of new products, attempts to reach different groups of customers, the need to offer new services, changes in promotional requirements, and stronger pressure on prices all tend to create situations in which new channels are explored. For a time, there may be instability in channels as new avenues are tried.

If companies are merely proliferating lines, as cigarette manufacturers or producers of grocery and drug products do, no channel changes are likely to be required. As diversification mergers and product expansion into unrelated fields bring about more "conglomerate" companies, however, channel additions and modifications become necessary.[9] Paint and margarine are not sold through the same channels nor are fountain pens and hearing aids, to mention just two of the kinds of marketing situations which have been created by mergers.

In addition to product and market changes, other changes in marketing strategy may have an impact on channels. The need to secure greater promotional and service support at the dealer level may result in a manufacturer shifting from general to selective distribution, perhaps through specific types of outlets. The need for greater selectivity in stocks may present an opportunity for new kinds of wholesalers, as in furniture and industrial equipment, or may encourage the manufacturer to set up his own wholesale branches.

A price squeeze in the channel may bring about some shifting of functions and perhaps a movement away from full-service wholesalers to such limited-function middlemen as drop shippers and cash-and-carry wholesalers. And long-term pressures of this type may destroy independent wholesale middlemen and replace them with integrated organizations such as voluntary chains and retailer cooperatives.

[8] Alexander and Berg, *op. cit.,* p. 272.

[9] The term "conglomerate" is applied to business combinations in which the parties involved were not competitors and did not occupy a customer-supplier relationship. (National Industrial Conference Board Report No. 93, p. 141.)

Selection of Trade Customers

Manufacturers who follow a policy of exclusive or selective distribution are faced with the problem of selecting the most suitable outlets to handle their lines. At least, the manufacturer can pick the middlemen he would *like* to have. Unless a manufacturer has such great prestige that most middlemen would be glad to carry his line, he may find that it is the middleman who is selective, and it may be difficult to interest leading wholesalers or retailers in the line. This occurs particularly when there are fewer good outlets in a city than there are leading manufacturers' lines. In such situations, distributors may appraise the lines offered quite carefully:

> Information that distributors sometimes use in appraising a potential supplier include: the manufacturer's record of financial capacity and stability; market potential for the supplier's product in the territory; major industries to be served by virtue of carrying the line; national and local sales position and reputation of the product line; national and local sales position of the supplier's major competitors; information on other distributors and dealers handling the line; sales policies of the company (e.g., terms, discounts, minimal inventory requirements, and total initial investment required); gross margin expectations; estimated annual sales volume, and profits for the first and succeeding years, should the line be added; warehousing requirements; packaging requirements for the product; advertising and sales promotion assistance; and field sales assistance and training available from the supplier.
>
> The manufacturer must be able to pass such an examination at least as well as his competitors if he is to succeed in adding the most desirable distributors to his reseller roster.[10]

Manufacturers may secure the names of potential outlets from several sources. The most important of these is usually the manufacturer's own field sales organization. Other leads come from distributors, trade directories, trade associations, trade shows, and direct inquiries from prospective outlets.

Leads may be screened informally or, preferably, by the use of checklists which permit a systematic evaluation of the firms being considered. The factors included may be ranked in order of importance, or subjective weights may be attached to them. In any case, evaluations will vary with the needs and experience of the manufacturer.

[10] Roger M. Pegram, *Selecting and Evaluating Distributors,* Business Policy Study No. 116, National Industrial Conference Board, 1965, p. 93.

Factors Governing Selection of Outlets

In the National Industrial Conference Board (NICB) survey, the most frequently used selection factor was the middleman's credit and financial standing.[11] Since financial stability is basic to good management and the growth of the business, it is not surprising that it ranks first. Most wholesalers and some dealers must be able to extend credit to their customers. Furthermore, such stability is necessary to minimize the manufacturer's risks in the venture. In various ways, the manufacturer makes an investment in a dealer or a distributor just as he makes an investment in his own personnel. Therefore, he is anxious that a strong, continuing relationship be developed and that the outlet steadily increase its influence in the market.

Along with financial stability, the capabilities of the middleman's management personnel are of major importance. Are they competent to handle all phases of the business? Are they growth-minded? Are they cooperative to the extent that they will work with the manufacturer? Has the firm developed a high reputation in the trade and among its customers? Has the firm a relatively young management or a group of younger people coming along who will be able to move into top management?

Among special capabilities, the marketing strategy of the firm has particular significance. Does it have a strong sales organization? Does it do an effective job of sales promotion? Are its price policies sound, and will it follow the manufacturer's suggestions in pricing? And in a closely related area, does the firm carry adequate stocks and is it capable of performing the necessary customer services?

The sales of a manufacturer's line will be affected by the other lines which the outlet carries, both allied and competitive. Therefore, the manufacturer is also interested in the nature and quality of these lines. The most desirable situation, from the manufacturer's point of view, is where the other lines are complementary to his rather than competitive. Manufacturers usually would prefer that outlets carry no lines competitive with theirs, but this is possible only under special circumstances.[12] If several good competing lines are available and the number of outlets

[11] *Ibid.*, p. 25.
[12] Outlets generally do not carry competitive lines of automobiles, petroleum products, and products distributed under franchise.

in an area is quite limited, the manufacturer may have to accept the fact that the outlet may carry competing lines. It does not follow from this, however, that the manufacturer should use competing outlets if they are not needed to get adequate distribution.

If the lines carried are not complementary, at least they should be compatible. Otherwise, the outlet will not be selling its lines to the same market segments. Thus, a manufacturer of electrical fittings would want to sell to electrical distributors, who carry complementary lines, and perhaps to hardware wholesalers, who carry compatible lines, but he might not find it profitable to sell through a general-line industrial distributor whose lines had quite different uses.

In addition to being concerned with the kinds of customers an outlet reaches, the manufacturer is also interested in the geographical market covered. Middlemen regularly cover a given area, and manufacturers who want complete market coverage need a distribution of middlemen whose trading areas fit together in jigsaw-puzzle fashion. Overlapping is inevitable, but at least the core areas should fit together.

The manufacturer can be said to have optimum distribution when his outlets are so located and in such number that he can reasonably expect to reach his sales potential throughout the market.

Evaluation of Distribution Outlets

The manufacturer who is dependent on a limited number of outlets needs some assurance that sales of his products through these outlets are adequate. Basic market-potential data, selected for their relationship to his own industry, will indicate what sales levels should be; and a continuing program of sales analysis will show where the weak spots in distribution are. Salesmen can be alerted to situations which need improvement, and they may be able to find ways to help middlemen increase sales. Distributor quotas may be established for control purposes, but any attempt at enforcement is likely to prove difficult.

Other factors related to sales performance may be analyzed. These include inventories carried, the number of salesmen handling the line, technical competence of salesmen and their attitudes and cooperation in sales-training programs conducted by the manufacturer, sales promotional support at the local level, and cooperation in various other sales-supporting activities undertaken by the manufacturer.

How effective the manufacturer's efforts will be in improving distributor-dealer performance depends in large part on the value of the line to the middleman and the alternative outlets, if any, available to the manufacturer. When the middleman carries competing lines and when the manufacturer has little choice but to use him, there is not much that can be done beyond trying to secure voluntary cooperation from the outlet.

In the opposite situation, when the franchise is highly valued by the distributor and others are seeking to secure it, the manufacturer can demand, and get, maximum cooperation and impose substantial controls.

Need for Feedback from Distributor-Dealer Organization

For channels in being, the manufacturer needs some indication of how well the channel is functioning and whether there are problems or incipient problems which may cause dissatisfaction among middlemen and users of the product. When manufacturers sell directly to consumers through a personal sales organization or some other promotional device, the results, as measured by sales, are quite readily apparent; and customer attitudes, in addition to being reflected in sales, are transmitted through the sales organization or directly to management by way of complaints, requests for adjustments, merchandise returns, etc.

When middlemen are used, performance is harder to check, and both their attitudes and the attitudes of their customers may be difficult to detect. Beyond the first step in the channel, sales data are not easy to secure. Ordinarily, a wholesaler will not furnish a manufacturer with detailed customer sales figures, and the subsequent sales of retailers are still another step removed. Under a policy of selective distribution, an outlet may supply a manufacturer with sales and inventory figures by product line. Retail sales in a manufacturer-wholesaler-retailer channel, however, probably will have to come from warranty cards (where these can be used) or from market surveys of the retail-audit or consumer-survey type.

Performance data other than sales usually have to come from the middleman's customers, probably from some type of questionnaire survey which covers such areas as promotional activity, installation and repair services and adjustments, merchandise availability, breadth and depth of stocks, delivery services, credit arrangements, price structure, and technical aid and counsel.

The feedback of performance data covering sales and service of both the manufacturer and his middlemen is highly useful but incomplete. Performance data need to be supplemented with attitudinal data in order to determine whether there are criticisms or dissatisfactions which may be reflected in poor channel relationships and reduced sales at a later date.

Where these situations are not brought directly to the attention of the manufacturer, they need to be detected through periodic attitude surveys, either formal or informal. Complaints which filter back to the manufacturer are one indication of possible problem situations. Conversations with dealers or buyers at trade shows or conventions are another avenue of communication. A formal attitude survey which covers a wide range of factors impinging on supplier-customer relations, and which is taken on a sample basis periodically, should give the manufacturer a reasonably accurate reading on relationships among the parties in the channel. Such a survey is likely to be most useful, however, when it covers units with which the manufacturer is in direct contact. Farther down the channel, this device will need to be handled with more care and probably will need to be tied in with some type of incentive.

Channel-decision Model

Faced with alternative channels and the need to make a choice among them, the manufacturer must attempt to evaluate the qualitative and quantitative factors discussed above. An analysis of the qualitative factors may indicate clearly that there is little if any choice available. This is most likely to occur when direct-to-user sales are indicated in industrial goods. The choice may be very narrow where direct sales to retailers are required by the type of product, the only alternative being operation by the manufacturer of his own retail outlets. For consumer goods in the convenience and shopping categories, a wider range of alternatives is usually available.

Once the feasible alternatives have been determined by an analysis of the qualitative factors, a more detailed quantitative analysis may be made to facilitate the final choice. This requires the manufacturer to identify and analyze user markets in terms of their location, needs, and buying patterns. He must estimate probable sales to these markets in light of competitive conditions, and he should also attempt to foresee the probable changes in market share in the years immediately ahead.

With these goals in mind, he is ready to assess the marketing job to be done. This requires an analysis of the specific functions to be performed in the channel and the unit and dollar quantities involved. Each function—selling, storage, delivery, credit, installation and repair, technical aid, etc.—must be analyzed in detail, and the probable costs of performing these services by alternative channels should be estimated. At this point, some of the qualitative factors related to the kind of service each party is in a position to give need to be reintroduced, particularly when the longer-run view is taken.

The manufacturer should now be in a position to decide how much of the work of the channel he is willing to assume and what parts of the job are to be handled by middlemen. Ideally, the functions to be performed by middlemen should be matched against proposed trade margins. However, the manufacturer may find that he does not have full control over margins because they may already have been established by competitors or by custom in the industry. In this situation, the manufacturer may decide that existing trade margins are too high in terms of the services being performed by middlemen and that it would be more profitable to perform these services himself. This, of course, is what has actually happened in many instances, particularly when manufacturers have taken over wholesalers' activities.

A model delineating this procedure is shown in Figure 8. The model assumes that certain information is available: user purchases now and in the next few years ahead; the costs of performing the necessary marketing functions by alternative channels; "reasonable" margins as related to channel functions performed; and qualitative performance data for channel middlemen. Much of the data must be in the nature of probabilities and estimates. Consequently, the manufacturer cannot expect the model to produce a precise, definitive answer. Probably there will be more than one answer, depending on the assumptions made.

This model has the advantages and limitations of most business-decision models. It contains the necessary parameters for analysis, and it does outline a specific procedure and workable alternatives. By following it, the manufacturer may, at least, be sure that he has taken all the significant variables into account and has systematically considered alternatives which otherwise might not have been included. The resulting decision should, therefore, be more rational in economic terms than a decision based on precedent or a casual consideration of some of the more obvious factors in the problem.

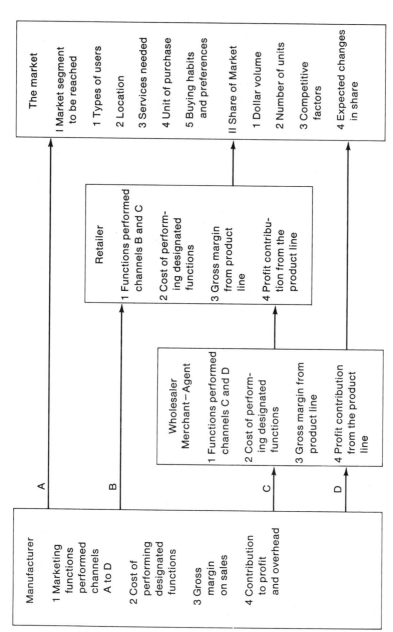

Figure 8 Channel-decision Model for a Manufacturer's Product Line

A similar approach to channel decisions is taken by Berg, who has devised the following five-step procedure:

(1) *Factoring the Strategic Situation.* Environmental factors and company resources are delineated; their impact on channels of distribution is indicated; and key factors are isolated.

(2) *Converting Key Factors into Activity Requirements*
Using the key factors determined in step (1), the activities to be performed by the units in the channel are established.

(3) *Grouping Tasks into Work Units*
Alternative methods of specialization are devised; and tasks are grouped for allocation to middlemen.

(4) *Allocating Tasks to Middlemen*
Markets to be served are segmented; alternative middlemen are identified; and tasks are assigned to channel units.

(5) *Designating Appropriate Structural Relationships*
The kinds of activities which need to be controlled are identified. Producers determine which activities they will attempt to control and which they will delegate to middlemen.[13]

Berg's procedure is somewhat more subjective than the model presented above. It may be more useful to small companies and to others who are not prepared to assemble the cost and performance information needed in the earlier model. Like the model, it does segment and systematize channel decisions.

Quantitative Channel-decision Techniques

In order to sharpen the decision-making process, some work has been done in the application of quantitative techniques to channel selection. Artle and Berglund presented a method for calculating functional channel costs for alternative channels together with the resulting sales and profit contribution.[14] Their analysis dealt only with personal selling costs and involved a comparison of selling through wholesalers and selling directly to retailers. However, their procedure could be applied to other functional costs and also to a wider range of channels.

Alderson and Green have applied Bayesian analysis to channel deci-

[13] Thomas L. Berg, "Designing the Distribution System," in William D. Stevens (ed.), *The Social Responsibilities of Marketing,* American Marketing Association, Chicago, 1962, pp. 481–490.
[14] Roland Artle and S. Berglund, "A Note on Manufacturers' Choice of Distribution Channels," *Management Science* (July, 1959).

sions. The specific example used is the replacement of company sales agents by its own sales force.[15] Comparative cost and sales data are estimated, and sales performance probabilities are established. The value and cost of securing both imperfect and perfect market information is also included.

Like all applications of the Bayesian method, this one depends on the ability of a firm to make satisfactory probability estimates. This part of the analysis can be improved with experience, however, and the Bayesian system has the merit of requiring the firm to identify and appraise the various outcomes associated with the channel decision. It also provides a mechanism for modifying original judgments by securing new information, and balances the costs of this information against its usefulness in reducing the costs arising from uncertainty.

Linear programming is another mathematical tool which can be used in areas related to channel decisions where the central question is one of allocating resources. Alderson and Green also present an example of linear programming procedures as applied to shipments from manufacturer to distributor warehouses where multiple locations are involved.[16]

For the analysis of market relationships which are too complex for subjective reasoning or for treatment in the limited-variable type of mathematical model, simulation procedures may offer some guidance. Computer simulation makes it possible to trace and study the impact of decisions made by the several parties in the simulation. The resulting insights into market interactions—the dynamics of a market—furnish a basis for making predictions concerning the probable impact of business decisions and the changing character of the market system.

Like other decision-making tools, computer simulation cannot incorporate all the variables which actually exist in any market, and it must operate within the established parameters. Nevertheless, it does have the merit of incorporating a substantial number of variables, perhaps all or most of the significant variables, together with reasonably realistic parameters. And it has the great advantage of numerous decision "runs" which serve to show the nature and timing of the interactions which occur.

Balderston and Hoggatt have used simulation to study the interrela-

---

[15] Wroe Alderson and Paul E. Green, *Planning and Problem Solving in Marketing,* Richard D. Irwin, Inc., Homewood, Ill., 1964, pp. 311–317.
[16] *Ibid.,* pp. 318–328.

tionships of channel participants in the West Coast lumber industry.[17] Lumber mills in this area sell to wholesalers, who sell in turn to retail lumber yards and industrial users. Wholesalers take the initiative in contacting both mills and their retailer-user customers. Transactions are usually carload lots which are drop-shipped to retailers or users, with wholesalers taking the credit risk and financing their customers.

The authors developed a very interesting and useful simulation methodology which covers the mill-wholesaler-retail lumber yard channel. The drop-shipment feature of the channel is incorporated, and the realistic assumption is made that communication up and down the channel is focused in the wholesaler. He undertakes the "searching" process among suppliers and retailers, arranges the transaction or order, and secures confirmation from both parties.

> At the end of each market period, each manufacturer uses decision-rules to set his offer price, output rate, and offer quantity on the market for the next period, and each retailer sets bid price, bid quantity, and retail price and sales quantity into the localized (and monopolistically competitive) final market facing him.
>
> At the end of each market period, insolvent firms (those having a negative cash position) go out of business. If average profits per firm in a certain class of participants are above an entry threshold, a new firm enters that class, up to the maximum limits specified for the number of members of each class.
>
> With probability less than one, each manufacturer and retailer adjusts physical plant upward or downward at the end of the market period to restore a desired ratio of plant to working capital.[18]

Considerably more work needs to be done in the application of quantitative techniques to channel decisions. The work which has been done in this area points the way to further research which should have fruitful results. Much needs to be learned, and while quantitative analysis cannot be expected to supply all the answers, there is enough evidence in hand to show that it can improve the channel decision–making process.

[17] Frederick Balderston and Austin Hoggatt, *Simulation of Market Processes,* Institute of Business and Economic Research, University of California Press, Berkeley, Calif., 1962.
[18] *Ibid.*

7

Theoretical
Explanations
of
Trade Channels

The previous chapters have traced the development of trade channels and the allocation of marketing functions within them, and have also examined the decision-making process involved in channels selection. As information concerning trade channels has grown, attempts have been made to explain the trade-channel phenomenon. Why do channels exist in a particular form, and what factors explain the changes which occur in channels?

Just as we do not have a complete body of marketing theory, neither do we have a complete explanation for the trade-channel structure and its workings. Some penetrating insights into trade channels have been presented, however, and these will be reviewed in the following pages.

Noting the differences among product channels and the basic patterns which seemed to evolve, Aspinwall devised the very useful "Characteristics of Goods and Parallel Systems Theories."[1] He departs from the earlier classification of goods into three categories (convenience, shopping, and specialty goods) and instead arranges goods along a continuous scale based on their marketing characteristics. The significant characteristics are those directly related to the trade channels used for the distribution of a product. They are five in number: (1) the replacement rate at which goods are bought, (2) the gross margin available to meet channel costs, (3) the services required by consumers, (4) the time involved in consumption, and (5) the "searching time" on the part of purchasers. When values are attached to the characteristics for each

[1] Leo Aspinwall, "The Characteristics of Goods and Parallel Systems Theories," in William Lazer and Eugene J. Kelley (eds.), *Managerial Marketing: Perspectives and Viewpoints,* Richard D. Irwin, Inc., Homewood, Ill., 1962, pp. 633–652.

product, the product sums vary as shown in Figure 9. The lower the total of the five characteristics, the longer the channel of distribution, and vice versa. A simplified classification is shown in Table 8.[2]

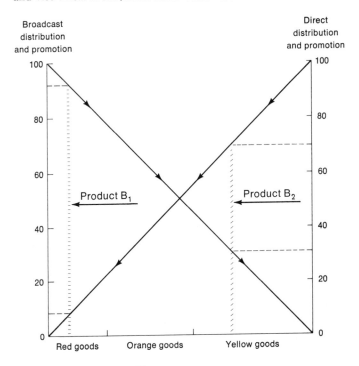

Figure 9 Parallel-Systems Theory
Goods are arrayed along the horizontal axis in terms of the sum of the designated product characteristics, low scores (red goods) to the left, high scores (yellow goods) to the right. A product located at the extreme right would be distributed entirely by direct distribution and promotion. A product designated B_2 would be distributed and promoted approximately 70 percent direct and 30 percent broadcast. One designated B_1 would be distributed and promoted about 92 percent broadcast and 8 percent direct. One at the far left would be sold entirely through broadcast channels and media.
SOURCE: Leo Aspinwall, "The Characteristics of Goods and Parallel Systems Theories," in William Lazer and Eugene J. Kelley (eds.), *Managerial Marketing: Perspectives and Viewpoints,* Richard D. Irwin, Homewood, Ill., 1962, p. 650.

2 Aspinwall has related his product continuum to the color spectrum. Thus, long-wave red goods have comparatively long channels, and shorter-wave yellow goods have the shortest channels. For simplicity, he has used only three colors rather than the full light spectrum.

Aspinwall's marketing characteristics are interrelated. As replacement increases, for example, the other factors decrease. Furthermore, his theory provides for the changes which occur over the product cycle.

> The position of a good on the color scale is not static. Most products fall in the yellow classification when they are first introduced. As they become better known and come to satisfy a wider segment of consumer demand, the replacement rate increases, and the good shifts toward the red end of the scale. . . . There is also an opposing tendency in marketing, however, resulting from the constant shrinking of gross margin as a good moves toward the red end of the scale. Marketing organizations in the effort to maintain their gross margin may improve or differentiate a good which has moved into the red category, so that some of these new varieties swing all the way back into yellow. Thereafter, the competitive drive for volume serves to accelerate the movement toward the red end of the scale again.[3]

TABLE 8

Characteristics of Goods

Marketing characteristics	Red goods	Orange goods	Yellow goods
Replacement rate	High	Medium	Low
Gross margin	Low	Medium	High
Services	Low	Medium	High
Time of consumption	Low	Medium	High
Searching time	Low	Medium	High

Source: Leo Aspinwall, "The Characteristics of Goods and Parallel Systems Theories," in William Lazer and Eugene J. Kelley (eds.), *Managerial Marketing: Perspectives and Viewpoints,* Richard D. Irwin, Inc., Homewood, Ill., 1962, pp. 633–652.

The parallel-systems theory is an extension of the characteristics-of-goods theory. Aspinwall shows that promotional methods are parallel to or match distribution channels. Long channels and general or "broadcast" promotional media go together, whereas short channels are matched by direct or "closed-circuit" promotion. The latter is typified by the direct contact involved in the sale of a custom-made product, while the former may be illustrated by the limited personal selling and

---

[3] Aspinwall, *op. cit.,* p. 643.

widespread use of mass advertising media found in the sale of convenience goods.

The Transvection Concept

Trade channels may be viewed in various ways, and several types of channels, therefore, have been identified. One of the major contributors to marketing theory, Wroe Alderson, believed that it is useful to consider the entire sequence of transactions from the raw-material stage through the final sale of a finished product. This may be necessary when an overall cost study is being made or when the efficiency of the whole vertical process from raw-material stage to finished product is being analyzed. Alderson used the term *transvection* to indicate the complete sequence from the sale of the raw material to the final sale of a finished product. The transvection sequence derives from the end sale.

> We are primarily concerned here with delineating a transvection which represents the shortest path to market, taking account of the several possible types of movement. . . . A transvection has the optimal number of steps if costs cannot be decreased either by increasing or decreasing the number of steps.[4]

In a concept one step removed from Alderson's idea of transvection, Professor Breyer states that the channel concept should be centered on a single product.[5] This idea is based on the observation that users buy individual products, each of which has different marketing characteristics.

Breyer points out that there are several ways of designating channels: *type* channels, which are identified only as certain kinds of businesses such as manufacturers, wholesale merchants, agents, retailers, etc.; *enterprise* channels, which consist of the specific firms in a given channel; *business unit* channels, which include different establishments or units under the same ownership (as, for example, a manufacturer's branch wholesale house); and *trading* channels, which are established when the arrangements underlying trade between buyer and seller have been

---

[4] Wroe Alderson and Miles W. Martin, "Toward a Formal Theory of Transactions and Transvections," *Journal of Marketing Research* (May, 1965), p. 125.
[5] Ralph F. Breyer, "Formation and Growth of Marketing Channels," in Reavis Cox, Wroe Alderson, and Stanley Shapiro (eds.), *Theory in Marketing: Second Series,* Richard D. Irwin, Inc., Homewood, Ill., 1964.

agreed upon. Presumably, trading channels exist once the agreement or contract indicating intent has been consumated. Goods may not actually move for some time, however, or they may move intermittently.

Marketing Flows

A broader way of looking at channels, which is also useful in terms of analyzing what marketing does and how well the job is done, is provided by the "flow" concept.[6] This concept is closely related to the marketing-functions approach. Several kinds of marketing flows may be identified: the physical movement of goods, the flow of goods through time (which involves the transfer of title), the flow of promotional activity to support and stimulate sales, the flow of credit, the distribution of risk, the flow of marketing information, and the flow of payment. Depending on the functional classifications one uses, other flows could be added to the list.

One of the significant features of the flow approach is that it recognizes that movement within a particular functional flow may be in either direction, as indicated in Figure 10. The flow of ownership and

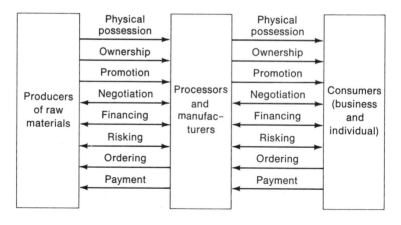

Figure 10 Flows in Marketing
source: Roland S. Vaile, E. T. Grether, and Reavis Cox, *Marketing in the American Economy,* The Ronald Press Company, New York, 1952, p. 113. Copyright 1952 by the publisher.

[6] R. S. Vaile, E. T. Grether, and Reavis Cox, *Marketing in the American Economy,* The Ronald Press Company, New York, 1952, p. 113.

promotion is from seller to buyer. The flow of payment is the reverse, and information may flow in either or both directions.

It is also apparent that the flow concept incorporates many kinds of institutions in addition to those primarily engaged in buying and selling: financial and credit institutions, insurance companies, transportation agencies, storage facilities, advertising agencies and media, marketing research organizations, and others.

The marketing flows concept is particularly useful in the analysis of complete marketing systems. This book has been concerned, however, with channels which facilitate the flow of title rather than those used for the performance of auxiliary marketing functions.

Market Separation Theory

Several theories have been developed to explain the complex channel structure which exists in the United States. One of these is the "gap" or "separation" theory.[7] McInnes states that the producer of a product is separated from users of the product in several ways. These types of separation are (1) geographical or spatial; (2) the time lapse between production and consumption; (3) the lack of perception and interest concerning the product on the part of potential buyers—"customers don't know about supply sources, producers don't know where customers are"; (4) the separation of ownership which exists until transfer of title has been completed; and (5) the separation in values: "If consumer capacity and willingness to pay, and producer capacity and willingness to offer differ greatly . . . it only makes the separation between the parties that much wider."

These five dimensions—space, time, perception, ownership, and valuation—form, according to McInnes, "the basic pattern that makes a market; they are the five dimensions of market potential that confront every marketing agent and determine every marketing institution . . . the existence of an institution should depend ultimately on the functions it performs in relation to the market potential it faces rather than on any other factor."[8]

It follows, therefore, that the channel structure (together with certain auxiliary agencies engaged in functions other than buying and selling)

[7] William McInnes, "A Conceptual Approach to Marketing," in Cox, Alderson, and Shapiro, *op. cit.*
[8] *Ibid.*, p. 59.

for any given product at a particular time will reflect the best arrangement to close these gaps. Marketing channels facilitate product "flows," and, in effect, serve as pipelines through which commodities move to market.

Depot Theory of Distribution

Goods do not flow through marketing channels uncontrolled, as a stream might move over its bed. Rather, they move at a controlled rate, and Professor Aspinwall in his depot theory of distribution states that "goods tend to move towards the point of final consumption at a rate established by the ultimate consumer." [9]

Aspinwall's thesis is that competitive pressures cause goods to be stored for a minimum period of time in the channel because of the investment and the storage costs involved. In an optimum situation, goods would flow steadily through the channel, merchandising (speculative) profits would be eliminated, storage and handling costs would be held to a minimum, and the sales price would reflect the basic commodity-handling services performed by middlemen.

The Sorting Concept

A particularly useful idea which gives considerable insight into the "whys" of marketing channels is the "sorting" concept.[10] As developed by Wroe Alderson, it includes four processes. The first, "sorting out," involves breaking a heterogeneous supply into separate lots through grading or inspection. The second, "accumulation," brings a number of like products together into a larger homogeneous supply, as when agricultural products are assembled in a local market for shipment in large quantities. This process of bringing together large stocks of similar products is called "concentration" by some authors.

The third aspect of sorting is "allocation" and consists of breaking down a homogeneous supply into smaller and smaller lots. This is also called "breaking bulk" by other writers when reference is made to the allocation activities of individual middlemen, especially wholesalers, and

[9] Leo V. Aspinwall, "The Depot Theory of Distribution," in W. Lazer and E. J. Kelley (eds.), *Managerial Marketing: Perspectives and Viewpoints*, Richard D. Irwin, Inc., Homewood, Ill., 1962, pp. 652–59.

[10] Wroe Alderson, "Factors Governing the Development of Marketing Channels," in R. M. Clewett (eds.), *Marketing Channels for Manufactured Products*, Richard D. Irwin, Inc., Homewood, Ill., 1954.

"dispersion" when refering to distribution over a wide geographical area.

The fourth type of sorting is "assorting" and involves building an assortment of different but perhaps related products to form a wholesaler's or retailer's stock.

It is a primary function of middlemen in the channel of distribution to perform these various sorting activities. Some, perhaps after grading or "sorting out," assemble like products into sizable quantities for shipment into a central market. Wholesalers of manufactured goods, on the other hand, assemble an "assortment" of diverse goods and, after breaking bulk, resell in smaller quantities, thus performing the third and fourth types of sorting.

Alderson used the term "technological distance" to indicate differences in the assortments of producers as compared with those of middlemen or users. At the producer level, assortments are dictated by production technology. At the consumer end, user assortments are governed by consumption patterns. These "discrepancies" in assortments create opportunities for middlemen to enter the channel of distribution. As goods move through the channel, assortments are changed by middlemen in such a way that the user can purchase the assortment required for his own needs most conveniently.

The technological assortment gap is thus bridged by the institutions in the channel. The sorting process aids in attaining greater efficiency in both the production and distribution of goods and creates opportunities for new forms of specialization within the channel. The discrepancy-of-assortments concept also explains why the successive stages in marketing are generally handled by independent agencies. The assortment gap places major limitations on vertical integration of marketing institutions, since most products involve different flows at each stage.

Wholesale and retail establishments ordinarily must carry the lines of more than one manufacturer in order to meet their customers' needs and to operate efficiently. A few manufacturers, in such fields as confectionery, shoes, and paper specialties, can integrate forward to the retail level without drawing merchandise from other suppliers. Manufacturers of tires, petroleum products, and shoes operate their own retail outlets but also sell at retail the products of other firms. These are exceptions to the general practice of having manufactured products handled by independent middlemen.

In the Alderson theory, the whole structure of channels rests on the concept of sorting. Intermediaries enter the channel when there are potential gains from additional sorting. When the cost of additional sorts is greater than the sorting benefits, and when channels of communication become too long and produce distorted messages, the influx of intermediaries stops.

The activities carried on between sorts involve the creation of time, place, or form utility; Alderson calls these changes "transformations." A transvection system extending back from the final sale of a product to the raw-material stage would involve a sequence of exchanges or title changes, based on resorting, and transformations. Such a sequence is shown below.

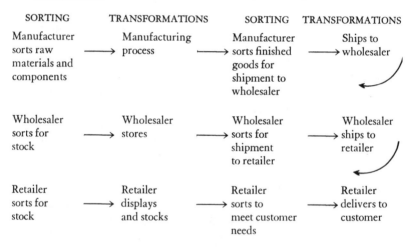

SORTING	TRANSFORMATIONS	SORTING	TRANSFORMATIONS
Manufacturer sorts raw materials and components	Manufacturing process	Manufacturer sorts finished goods for shipment to wholesaler	Ships to wholesaler
Wholesaler sorts for stock	Wholesaler stores	Wholesaler sorts for shipment to retailer	Wholesaler ships to retailer
Retailer sorts for stock	Retailer displays and stocks	Retailer sorts to meet customer needs	Retailer delivers to customer

The optimum number of steps in a transvection system is attained when costs cannot be further reduced by changing the number of steps.

Concept of Postponement

A corollary theory to sorting is the concept of *postponement*. The efficiency of a transvection system is maximized by postponing "changes in form and identity to the latest possible point in the marketing flow" and postponing "changes in inventory location to the latest possible point in time." [11] In effect, this concept involves gaining economies by

[11] Wroe Alderson, *Marketing Behavior and Executive Action,* Richard D. Irwin, Inc., Homewood, Ill., 1957, p. 424.

delaying differentiation of the product as long as possible. It is most efficient to sort in large lots before the product has become highly differentiated. The closer a product moves to the final user, the more differentiated it becomes. The greater the degree of differentiation, the higher are the risks of buying and stocking the product.

Bucklin suggests that the concept of postponement needs modification. "The principle which states that changes in form and inventory location are to be delayed to the latest possible moment, must also explain why in many channels these changes appear at the earliest." [12] The modification he presents is the "principle of speculation." This "principle" holds that "changes in form, and the movement of goods to forward inventories, should be made at the earliest possible time in the marketing flow in order to reduce the costs of the marketing system." This point of view is the reverse of the concept of postponement and is based on the opportunities for lower cost arising from making changes while quantities are still comparatively large.

The result is a combined "principle of postponement-speculation. . . . A speculative inventory will appear at each point in the distribution channel whenever its costs are less than the net savings to both buyer and seller from postponement." [13]

This "principle" is not inconsistent with Aspinwall's depot theory, which was mentioned earlier. In convenience goods (groceries, drugs, tobacco products, hardware) it is probable that the depot theory tends to operate. In other fields, furniture for example, the working of Bucklin's theory can be seen; and we find that the need for speculative inventories presents an opportunity for new types of wholesalers. Retailers wish to shift the inventory risk backward but still have stocks fairly close at hand. This then creates an opening for a merchant wholesaler. Likewise, wholesalers in some fields, such as frozen foods, tobacco products, and electrical wire and cable, may prefer to carry low inventories. This causes manufacturers to carry regional field stocks either in their own warehouses or in public warehouses.

Bucklin developed several hypotheses in connection with his postponement-speculation concept:

1. The shorter the delivery time, the greater the probability the channel will include an intermediate, speculative inventory.

---

[12] Louis P. Bucklin, "Postponement, Speculation and the Structure of Distribution Channels," *Journal of Marketing Research* (February, 1965), p. 27.
[13] *Ibid.*, p. 28.

2. The shorter the delivery time, the closer any speculative stock will be to the consumer.
3. The shorter the distance between a customer and a speculative stock, the greater the probability of a second such inventory in the channel.
4. Products which are heavy, bulky, and inexpensive are likely to flow through channels with more intermediate, speculative inventories than products with the opposite characteristics.
5. Products which consumers find expensive to store on their premises, but whose use is both urgent and difficult to forecast, have a greater probability of passing through an intermediate, speculative inventory than products with the opposite characteristics.
6. The greater the inelasticity of consumer and/or producer cost with respect to changes in delivery time, the greater the stability of the most efficient channel-type over time.[14]

Conditions Underlying Need for Middlemen

The simplest form of distribution is for producers to sell directly to consumers. In order for middlemen to find a niche in a trade channel, they must perform certain of the marketing functions in such a way that savings result or satisfactions are greater for each of the original parties. In a marginal situation, the introduction of a middleman should produce results for producer and consumer which are no less favorable than those which existed prior to his entrance. Furthermore, for his niche to be satisfactory, he must eventually make a profit.

Baligh and Richartz have examined the circumstances which favor the intervention of middlemen. In their analysis, the component economic activities are split into two groups: those which precede the receipt of an order, which are called "preorder production activities," and those performed subsequently, which are labeled "postorder production activities." The activities associated with physical production ordinarily are carried on prior to the receipt of an order; those included in marketing occur both before and after the order is placed. By using a model which involves a single-product structure with no change in the flow of orders, and assuming that middlemen are operating at one level and that their number is less than the number of initial sellers, the authors conclude that (1) the total resources used by all firms in preorder production are greater than when no middlemen are used, since middlemen convert

[14] *Ibid.*, p. 30.

inventories into a form nearer that required by consumers (this is an extension of Alderson's sorting concept); (2) the total resources devoted to postorder production activities (essentially marketing activities) are less when middlemen are used; (3) as the number of middlemen at the given level is increased beyond the point where they incur competitive costs, the efficiency of the system is reduced.[15]

The middleman must optimize his allocation of preorder production and postorder production activities in order to find a place in the channel, and he must also determine an optimum level of product form. Under the simplified terms of the model, he can then make a contribution to channel efficiency. Alderson's principle of postponement and Bucklin's principle of speculation can also be tied to the model and to the conclusions based on it.

Dynamics of Marketing Channels

The preceding chapters have shown that both the institutional structure of marketing and the functions performed by the various parties in the channel are highly dynamic. In our economy there is constant competition among many kinds of businesses for the opportunity to perform the various functions of distribution. It is also apparent that the needs and desires of consumers are constantly changing, and this puts new demands on the structure and creates new opportunities.

At any moment in time, the marketing structure is in an uneasy state of equilibrium. Innovators are constantly at work, and producers, wholesalers, and retailers are experimenting with changes in the mix of functions and the manner in which they are performed. There is an underlying order in trade channels, however, of a flexible and gradually changing type. Under the free-enterprise system, entrepreneurs are on the alert for ways of altering the "package" of goods and services offered to buyers, and for ways of recombining marketing functions.

In most parts of the world, the marketing structure has had a high

---

[15] Adapted from Helmy H. Baligh and Leon Richartz, "Some Considerations on the Performance of Economic Activities of Intermediaries," *Science, Technology, and Marketing,* American Marketing Association, Chicago, 1967.

The authors have developed their ideas concerning vertical market structure equilibrium more fully in a recent book, *Vertical Market Structures,* Allyn and Bacon, Inc., Boston, 1967. In it they develop more complex models which incorporate situations involving multiproducts, multimarket segments, and specialization within channels.

degree of stability, with the trade channels of some industries remaining unchanged for decades. Many of the trade channels outlined in Chapter 3 have survived for very long periods, especially in the underdeveloped countries. In the United States, however, the changes have been comparatively rapid. In the ever-present drive for higher profits, innovators at all levels have sought improvements; and the status and growth patterns of the several types of middlemen have gradually changed.

There is every indication that trade channels will continue to evolve and to become attuned to the shifts in goods and services desired by the several types of buyers in the market. Both our business system and the legal constraints within which business operates serve to encourage innovators. Consequently, as long as entry barriers are held to a minimum and profit incentives are maintained, the business community may be expected to search for more effective methods of distribution.

Bibliography

Books and Monographs

ADDISON, WILLIAM, *English Fairs and Markets,* B. T. Batsford Ltd., London, 1953.

ALDERSON, WROE, *Dynamic Marketing Behavior,* Richard D. Irwin, Inc., Homewood, Ill., 1965.

——, *Marketing Behavior and Executive Action,* Richard D. Irwin, Inc., Homewood, Ill., 1957.

—— and PAUL E. GREEN, *Planning and Problem Solving in Marketing,* Richard D. Irwin, Inc., Homewood, Ill., 1964.

ALEXANDER, RALPH S., and THOMAS L. BERG, *Dynamic Management in Marketing,* Richard D. Irwin, Inc., Homewood, Ill., 1965, chap. 10.

——, JAMES S. CROSS, and RICHARD M. HILL, *Industrial Marketing,* Richard D. Irwin, Inc., Homewood, Ill., 1967, chaps. 9 and 10.

AMES, J. W., *Cooperative Sweden Today,* Co-operative Union, Manchester, England, 1952.

BAKKEN, HENRY H., *Theory of Markets and Marketing,* Mimir Publishers, Madison, Wis., 1953.

BALDERSTON, FREDERICK E., and AUSTIN C. HOGGART, *Simulation of Market Processes,* Institute of Business and Economic Research, University of California Press, Berkeley, Calif., 1962.

BALDWIN, K. D., *Marketing of Cocoa in Western Nigeria,* Oxford University Press, Fair Lawn, N.J., 1954.

BALIGH, HEMLY H., and LEON E. RICHARTZ, *Vertical Market Structures,* Allyn and Bacon, Inc., Boston, 1967.

BARGER, HAROLD, *Distribution's Place in the American Economy since 1869,* Princeton University Press, Princeton, N.J., 1955.

BARTELS, ROBERT (ed.), *Comparative Marketing: Wholesaling in Fifteen Countries,* Richard D. Irwin, Inc., Homewood, Ill., 1962.

BOHANNAN, PAUL (ed.), *Markets in Africa,* Northwestern University Press, Evanston, Ill., 1962.

BONNER, ARNOLD, *British Cooperation,* Cooperative Union, Holyoake House, Manchester, England, 1961.

BRELSFORD, WILLIAM V., *Copperbelt Markets: A Social and Economic Study,* Government Printer, Lusaka, Northern Rhodesia, 1947.

BREYER, RALPH F., *Commodity Marketing,* McGraw-Hill Book Company, New York, 1931.

———, *The Marketing Institution,* McGraw-Hill Book Company, New York, 1934.

———, *Quantitative Systemic Analysis and Control: Study No. 1, Channel and Channel Group Costing,* College Offset Press, Philadelphia, 1949.

BRION, JOHN M., *Marketing through the Wholesaler/Distributor Channel,* American Marketing Association, Chicago, 1965.

BUCKLIN, LOUIS P., *A Theory of Distribution Channel Structure,* Graduate School of Business Administration, University of California, Berkeley, Calif., 1966.

BUZZELL, ROBERT D., *Value Added by Industrial Distributors,* Bureau of Business Research, Ohio State University, Columbus, Ohio, 1959.

CARSON, DAVID, *International Marketing: A Comparative Systems Approach,* John Wiley & Sons, Inc., New York, 1967.

CASSADY, RALPH JR., and WYLIE L. JONES, *The Changing Competitive Structure in the Wholesale Grocery Trade,* University of California Press, Berkeley, Calif., 1949.

CLEWETT, RICHARD M. (ed.), *Marketing Channels for Manufactured Products,* Richard D. Irwin, Inc., Homewood, Ill., 1954.

COLE, ROBERT, *Vertical Integration in Marketing,* College of Commerce and Business Administration, University of Illinois, Urbana, Ill., 1952.

COX, REAVIS, and WROE ALDERSON (eds.), *Theory in Marketing,* Richard D. Irwin, Inc., Homewood, Ill., 1950.

———, WROE ALDERSON, and STANLEY SHAPIRO (eds.), *Theory in Marketing: Second Series,* Richard D. Irwin, Inc., Homewood, Ill., 1964.

———, CHARLES GOODMAN, and THOMAS FICHANDLER, *Distribution in a High-level Economy,* Prentice-Hall, Inc., Englewood Cliffs, N.J., 1965.

DACCA (Pakistan) UNIVERSITY, Socio-economic Research Board, *Marketing of Jute in East Pakistan,* Oxford University Press, Fair Lawn, N.J., 1961.

DAVISSON, CHARLES N., *The Marketing of Automotive Parts,* Bureau of Business Research, University of Michigan, Ann Arbor, Mich., 1954.

DAY, CLIVE, *A History of Commerce,* Longmans, Green & Co., Inc., (David McKay Company, Inc.), New York, 1938.

DEWEY, ALICE G., *Peasant Marketing in Java,* The Free Press of Glencoe (The Macmillan Company), New York, 1962.

DEWHURST, J. FREDERIC, et al., *Europe's Needs and Resources,* The Twentieth Century Fund, New York, 1961.

DIAMOND, WILLIAM M., *Distribution Channels for Industrial Goods,* Bureau of Business Research, Ohio State University, Columbus, Ohio, 1964.

DUDDY, EDWARD A., and DAVID A. REVZAN, *Marketing: An Institutional Approach,* McGraw-Hill Book Company, New York, 1953.

FISK, GEORGE, *Marketing Systems: An Introductory Analysis,* Harper & Row, Publishers, Incorporated, New York, 1967.

FULOP, CHRISTINA, *Competition for Consumers: A Study of Changing Channels of Distribution,* Institute of Economic Affairs, London, 1964.

GALBRAITH, JOHN K., *American Capitalism,* Houghton Mifflin Company, Boston, 1956.

—— and RICHARD H. HOLTON, *Marketing Efficiency in Puerto Rico,* Harvard University Press, Cambridge, Mass., 1955.

GOLDMAN, MARSHALL I., *Soviet Marketing: Distribution in a Controlled Economy,* The Free Press of Glencoe (The Macmillan Company), New York, 1963.

GUPTA, RANJIT, *Retailing in Metropolitan India,* Indian Cooperative Union, New Delhi, 1964.

HALL, MARGARET, *Distributive Trading,* Hutchinson's University Library, London, 1944.

——, JOHN KNAPP, and CHRISTOPHER WINSTON, *Distribution in Great Britain and North America,* Oxford University Press, Fair Lawn, N.J., 1962.

HAWKINS, H. C. G., *Wholesale and Retail Trade in Tanganyika,* F. A Praeger, New York, 1965.

HECKERT, J. B., and R. E. MINER, *Distribution Cost Accounting,* The Ronald Press Company, New York, 1953.

HIRSCH, LEON V., *Marketing in an Underdeveloped Economy: The North Indian Sugar Industry,* Prentice-Hall, Inc., Englewood Cliffs, N.J., 1961.

HOLDREN, BOB R., *The Structure of a Retail Market and the Market*

Behavior of Retail Units, Prentice-Hall, Inc., Englewood Cliffs, N.J., 1960.

HOLLANDER, STANLEY, *Explorations in Retailing,* Bureau of Business and Economic Research, Michigan State University, East Lansing, Mich., 1959.

HOTCHKISS, GEORGE BURTON, *Milestones of Marketing,* The Macmillan Company, New York, 1938.

JEFFERYS, JAMES B., *The Distribution of Consumer Goods,* Cambridge University Press, New York, 1950.

——, *Retail Trading in Britain: 1850–1950,* Cambridge University Press, New York, 1954.

—— and DEREK KNEE, *Retailing in Europe,* St. Martin's Press, New York, 1962.

JONES, FRED, *Middlemen in the Domestic Trade of the United States 1800–1860,* Illinois Studies in the Social Sciences, The University of Illinois Press, Urbana, Ill., 1937.

KACKER, M. P., *Marketing of Cotton Price Goods in India,* Vora, Bombay, India, 1962.

KOTLER, PHILIP, *Marketing Management,* Prentice-Hall, Inc., Englewood Cliffs, N.J., 1967, chap. 16.

LAZO, HECTOR, and ARNOLD CORBIN, *Management in Marketing,* McGraw-Hill Book Company, New York, 1961, chap. 9.

LEBHAR, GODFREY M., *Chain Stores in America, 1859–1950,* Chain Store Publishing Corporation, New York, 1952.

LEVY, HERMANN, *The Shops of Britain,* Oxford University Press, Fair Lawn, N.J., 1947.

LEWIS, EDWIN H., *Marketing Electrical Apparatus and Supplies,* McGraw-Hill Book Company, New York, 1961.

——, *Wholesaling in the Twin Cities,* The University of Minnesota Press, Minneapolis, 1952.

—— and ROBERT S. HANCOCK, *The Franchise System of Distribution,* University of Minnesota, Minneapolis, 1963.

LONGMAN, D. R., and M. SCHIFF, *Practical Distribution Cost Analysis,* Richard D. Irwin, Inc., Homewood, Ill., 1955.

McNAIR, MALCOLM P., and ELEANOR G. MAY, *The American Department Store (1920–1960),* Graduate School of Business Administration, Harvard University, Cambridge, Mass., 1963.

APPLEBAUM, WILLIAM, and S. B. COHEN, "Trading Area Networks and Problems of Store Saturation," *Journal of Retailing* (Winter, 1961–1962), pp. 32–43, 55.

ARTLE, ROLAND, and S. BERGLUND, "A Note on Manufacturers' Choice of Distribution Channel," *Management Science* (July, 1959), pp. 460–471.

ASPINWALL, LEO, "The Characteristics of Goods and Parallel Systems Theories," in William Lazer and Eugene J. Kelley (eds.), *Managerial Marketing: Perspectives and Viewpoints,* Richard D. Irwin, Inc., Homewood, Ill., 1962, pp. 633–652; also "The Depot Theory of Distribution," pp. 652–659.

BAKER, RAYMOND W., "Marketing in Nigeria," *Journal of Marketing* (July, 1965), pp. 40–48.

BALDERSTON, F. E., "Communication Networks in Intermediate Markets," *Management Science* (January, 1958), pp. 154–171.

———, "Theories of Marketing Structure and Channels," in *Proceedings: Conference of Marketing Teachers from Far Western States,* University of California, Berkeley, September, 1958, pp. 134–145.

———, "Analytic Models versus Computer Simulation—A Comparison with Illustrations from the Lumber Trade," in *Marketing Concepts in Changing Times,* American Marketing Association, Chicago, 1960, pp. 139–151.

BANKS, SEYMOUR, "Comments on Alderson's Index of Sorting Balance," *Journal of Marketing* (January, 1951), pp. 331–335.

BAUER, P. T., "Concentration in Tropical Trade: Some Aspects and Implications of Oligopoly," *Economica: New Series* (November, 1953), pp. 302–321.

BAUMOL, WILLIAM J., and E. A. IDE, "Variety in Retailing," *Management Science* (October, 1956), pp. 93–101.

BENNETT, PETER D., "Retailing Evolution or Revolution in Chile?" *Journal of Marketing* (July, 1966), pp. 38–41.

BERG, THOMAS L., "Designing the Distribution System," in William D. Stevens (ed.), *The Social Responsibilities of Marketing,* American Marketing Association, Chicago, 1962, pp. 481–90.

BOYD, HARPER W., JR., RICHARD M. CLEWETT, and RALPH L. WESTFALL, "The Marketing Structure of Venezuela," *Journal of Marketing* (April, 1958), pp. 391–397.

———, ABDEL AZIZ EL SHERBINI, and AHMED FOUAD SHERIF, "Channels of Distribution for Consumer Goods in Egypt," *Journal of Marketing* (October, 1961), pp. 26–33.

――― and IVAN PIERCY, "Retailing in Great Britain," *Journal of Marketing* (January, 1963), pp. 29–35.

――― and ―――, "Marketing to the British Consumer," *Business Horizons* (Spring, 1963), pp. 77–86.

BUCKLIN, LOUIS P., "The Economic Structure of Channels of Distribution," in *Marketing: A Maturing Discipline,* American Marketing Association, Chicago, 1960, pp. 379–385.

―――, "Retail Strategy and the Classification of Consumer Goods," *Journal of Marketing* (January, 1963), pp. 51–56.

―――, "Postponement, Speculation, and the Structure of Distribution Channels," *Journal of Marketing Research* (February, 1965), pp. 26–31.

――― and LESLIE HALPERT, "Explaining Channels of Distribution for Cement with the Principle of Postponement Speculation," in *Economic Growth, Competition, and World Markets,* American Marketing Association, Chicago, 1965, pp. 696–709.

BURSK, EDWARD C., "View Your Customers as Investments," *Harvard Business Review* (May–June, 1966), pp. 91–94.

BUZZELL, ROBERT B., and CHARLES C. SLATER, "Decision Theory and Marketing Management," *Journal of Marketing* (July, 1962), pp. 7–16.

CARSON, DAVID, "Marketing in Italy Today," *Journal of Marketing* (January, 1966), pp. 10–16.

CHRISTIAN, RICHARD C., "Industrial Marketing: Three Step Method to Better Distribution Channel Analysis," *Journal of Marketing* (October, 1958), pp. 191–192.

COLLINS, A. L., "Warehouse Distribution of Steel," *Journal of Marketing* (September, 1949), pp. 358–361.

CONVERSE, PAUL D., "Twenty-five Years of Wholesaling: A Revolution in Food Wholesaling," *Journal of Marketing* (July, 1957), pp. 40–53.

COPELAND, MELVIN T., "Relation of Consumers' Buying Habits to Marketing Methods," *Harvard Business Review* (April, 1923), pp. 282–289.

COX, REAVIS, "The Channel of Marketing as a Unit of Competition," in W. D. Robbins (ed.), *Successful Marketing at Home and Abroad,* American Marketing Association, Chicago, 1958, pp. 208–212.

———, "Consumer Convenience and the Retail Structure of Cities," *Journal of Marketing* (April, 1959), pp. 355–362.

———, "Changes in the City as an Institution of Marketing," in *Marketing Adjustment to the Environment,* American Marketing Association, Chicago, 1962.

——— and C. S. Goodman, "Marketing of House-building Materials," *Journal of Marketing* (July, 1956), pp. 36–61.

Craig, David R., and Warner K. Gabler, "The Competitive Struggle for Market Control," in *The Annals of the American Academy of Political and Social Science* (May, 1940), pp. 84–107.

Cundiff, Edward W., "Concepts in Comparative Retailing," *Journal of Marketing,* (January, 1965), pp. 59–63.

Dale, Ernest, "The Changing Channels of Distribution: Lower Costs, New Freedom for Consumers," *Printers' Ink* (July 11, 1958), pp. 21–27.

Darling, S. L., "The Lumber Wholesaler," *Journal of Marketing* (September, 1949), pp. 349–354.

Davidson, William R., "Channels of Distribution—One Aspect of Marketing Strategy," *Business Horizons* (February, 1961), pp. 84–90.

DeLoach, D. B., "Competition for Channel Control in the Food Industry," in *Proceedings: Conference of Marketing Teachers from Far Western States,* University of California, Berkeley (September, 1958), pp. 119–128.

de Salaberry, Louis, "How Suppliers Can Reach Germany's Big Purchasers," *International Commerce* (Nov. 26, 1962), pp. 10–11.

Douglas, Edna, "Size of Firm and the Structure of Costs in Retailing," *Journal of Business* (April, 1962), pp. 158–190.

Dowd, Laurence P., "Wholesale Marketing in Japan," *Journal of Marketing* (January, 1959), pp. 257–262.

Dunn, S. Watson, "French Retailing and the Common Market," *Journal of Marketing* (January, 1962), pp. 19–22.

Edwards, C. D., "The Struggle for the Control of Distribution," *Journal of Marketing* (January, 1937), pp. 212–217.

———, "Vertical Integration and the Monopoly Problem," *Journal of Marketing* (April, 1953), pp. 404–410.

Elgass, George A., "Marketing in Japan: An Expanding Economy," in William D. Stevens (ed.), *The Social Responsibilities of Marketing,* American Marketing Association, Chicago, 1962, pp. 425–433.

ENTENBERG, ROBERT D., "Suggested Changes in Census Classifications of Retail Trade," *Journal of Marketing* (January, 1960), pp. 39–43.

EVANS, KEITH J., "When and How Should You Sell through Distributors," *Industrial Marketing* (March, 1959), pp. 41–44.

EVELY, R. W., "Distribution Methods and Costs in the U.S.A.," *Review of Economic Studies,* 1946, pp. 16–33.

EWING, JOHN S., "Marketing in Australia," *Journal of Marketing* (April, 1962), pp. 54–58.

———, "Discount Houses in Australia and Mexico," *Journal of Marketing* (July, 1962), pp. 37–41.

FOSTER, GEORGE M., "The Folk Economy of Rural Mexico with Special Reference to Marketing," *Journal of Marketing* (October, 1948), pp. 153–162.

FUKAMI, GIICHI, "Japanese Department Stores," *Journal of Marketing* (July, 1953), pp. 41–49.

"Germany's Retail Trade Agitated by Inroads of Discount Houses," *International Commerce* (Nov. 26, 1962), pp. 15–16.

GILCHRIST, FRANK W., "The Discount House," *Journal of Marketing* (January, 1953), pp. 57–59.

GILLESPIE, S. C., and K. W. ROTHSCHILD, "Migration and the Distributive Trades," *Review of Economic Studies,* 1946, pp. 81–83.

GIRDNER, WILLIAM, "Integrated Marketing Institutions," in *The Annals of the American Academy of Political and Social Science,* Philadelphia (May, 1940), pp. 55–61.

GOLDMAN, MARSHALL I., "Retailing in the Soviet Union," *Journal of Marketing* (April, 1960), pp. 9–15.

———, "The Marketing Structure in the Soviet Union," *Journal of Marketing* (July, 1961), pp. 7–14.

GOLDSTUCKER, JAC L., "Marketing in Great Britain," in *Doing Business with Great Britain,* DePaul University, Chicago, 1966, pp. 26–42.

GRANBOIS, DONALD H., and RONALD P. WILLETT, "Patterns of Conflicting Perceptions among Channel Members," in L. George Smith (ed.), *Reflections on Progress in Marketing,* American Marketing Association, Chicago, 1964, pp. 86–100.

GREENHUT, M. L., "The Size and Shape of the Market Area of a Firm," *Southern Economic Journal* (July, 1952), pp. 37–50.

GRETHER, E. T., "Solidarity in the Distribution Trades," *Law and Contemporary Problems* (June, 1937), pp. 376–391.

GUERIN, JOSEPH R., "Limitations of Supermarkets in Spain," *Journal of Marketing* (October, 1964), pp. 22–26.

HALL, WILLIAM P., "Franchising—New Scope for an Old Technique," *Harvard Business Review* (January–February, 1964), pp. 60–72.

HANSEN, RICHARD W., "The Growth and Development of Cooperative Retail Chains and Their Marketing Significance," in L. George Smith (ed.), *Reflections on Progress in Marketing,* American Marketing Association, Chicago, 1964, pp. 110–118.

HEFLEBOWER, R. B., "Mass Distribution: A Phase of Bilateral Oligopoly or of Competition," in *American Economic Association Papers and Proceedings* (December, 1956), pp. 274–285.

HERR, WILLIAM McD., "The Changing Australian Food Industry," *Journal of Marketing* (April, 1963), pp. 23–26.

HETTINGER, HERMAN S., "Marketing in Persia," *Journal of Marketing* (January, 1951) pp. 289–297.

HEWITT, CHARLES H., "The Furor over Dealer Franchises," *Business Horizons* (Winter, 1958), pp. 80–87.

HOLLANDER, STANLEY C., "The Discount House," *Journal of Marketing* (July, 1953), pp. 57–59.

——, "The Wheel of Retailing," *Journal of Marketing* (July, 1960), pp. 37–42.

HOLTON, RICHARD H., "Marketing Structure and Economic Development," *Quarterly Journal of Economics* (August, 1953), pp. 344–361.

HOWARD, M. C., "Interfirm Relations in Oil Products Markets," *Journal of Marketing* (April, 1956), pp. 356–366.

JACK, A. B., "The Channels of Distribution for an Innovation: The Sewing Machine Industry in America, 1860–65," *Explorations in Entrepreneurial History* (February, 1957), pp. 58–60.

KANE, JAMES F., "Marketing Behavior and the Environment: An Ecological Study of the Adaptive Behavior of Marketing Agencies," in L. George Smith (ed.), *Reflections on Progress in Marketing,* American Marketing Association, Chicago, 1964, pp. 101–109.

KATZIN, MARGARET, "The Role of the Small Entrepreneur," in Melville J. Herskovits and Mitchell Horwitz (eds.), *Economic Transition in Africa,* Northwestern University Press, Evanston, Ill., 1964.

KESSLER, FRIEDRICH, NEWTON D. BRENNER, and RICHARD H. STERN, "Automobile Dealer Franchises: Vertical Integration by Contract," *The Yale Law Journal,* 1959, pp. 1–129.

KOHLS, R. L., "Decision Making in Integrated Production and Marketing Systems," *Journal of Farm Economics* (December, 1958), pp. 1801–1811.

Konopa, Leonard J., "What Is Meant by Franchise Selling?" *Journal of Marketing* (April, 1963), pp. 35–37.

Koo, A. Y. C., "A Theoretical Note on the Dealer-Manufacturer Relationship in the Automobile Industry," *Quarterly Journal of Economics* (May, 1959), pp. 316–325.

LAMBERT, EUGENE W., JR., "Financial Considerations in Choosing a Marketing Channel," *Business Topics,* Michigan State University, East Lansing (Winter, 1966), pp. 17–26.

LEWIS, EDWIN H., "Wholesale Market Patterns," *Journal of Marketing* (January, 1948), pp. 317–326.

———, "Comeback of the Wholesaler," *Harvard Business Review* (November–December, 1955), pp. 115–125.

———, "Marketing in Spain," *Journal of Marketing* (October, 1964), pp. 17–21.

LIVESEY, C. A., "The Steel Warehouse Distributor," *Harvard Business Review* (Spring, 1947), p. 397.

LUDERS, ROLF J., and ALLEN F. JUNG, "Retail Competition," *Journal of Marketing* (April, 1964), pp. 22–24.

McCAMMON, BERT C., JR., "Alternative Explanations of Institutional Change and Channel Evolution," in *Toward Scientific Marketing,* American Marketing Association, Chicago (December, 1963), pp. 477–490.

——— and ALBERT D. BATES, "The Emergence and Growth of Contractually Integrated Channels in the American Economy," in P. D. Bennett (ed.), *Economic Growth, Competition, and World Markets,* American Marketing Association, Chicago, 1965, pp. 496–515.

——— and ROBERT W. LITTLE, "Marketing Channels: Analytical Systems and Approaches," in George Schwartz (ed.), *Science in Marketing,* John Wiley & Sons, Inc., New York, 1965, pp. 321–385.

McCLELLAND, W. G., "Costs and Competition, British Style," in *Proceedings of the Boston Conference on Distribution,* Retail Trade Board, Boston Chamber of Commerce, 1961.

McFARLAND, S. W., "The Marketing Position of Industrial Distributors," *Journal of Marketing* (April, 1953), pp. 394–403.

McGarry, Edmund D., "The Contactual Function in Marketing," *Journal of Business* (April, 1953), pp. 96–113.

——, "Some Viewpoints in Marketing," *Journal of Marketing* (July, 1953), p. 36.

——, "The Propaganda Function in Marketing," *Journal of Marketing* (October, 1958), pp. 131–139.

McNair, Malcolm P., "Significant Trends and Developments in the Postwar Period," in *Competitive Distribution in a Free High-level Economy and Its Implications for the University,* The University of Pittsburgh Press, Pittsburgh, Pa., 1958, pp. 1–25.

McVey, Phillip, "Are Channels of Distribution What the Textbooks Say?" *Journal of Marketing* (January, 1960), pp. 61–65.

Mallen, Bruce, "A Theory of Retailer-Supplier Conflict, Control and Cooperation," *Journal of Retailing* (Summer, 1963), pp. 24–32.

——, "Conflict and Cooperation in Marketing Channels," in L. George Smith (ed.), *Reflections on Progress in Marketing,* American Marketing Association, Chicago, 1964, pp. 65–85.

——, "Introducing the Marketing Channel to Price Theory," *Journal of Marketing* (July, 1964), pp. 29–33.

Marcus, Edward, "Selling the Tropical African Market," *Journal of Marketing* (July, 1961), pp. 25–31.

Marcus, Mildred R., "Merchandise Distribution in Tropical Africa," *Journal of Retailing* (Winter, 1960), pp. 197ff.

Marino, John A., "Japan's Trading Companies," *Boston University Business Review* (Spring, 1965).

Meyer, Charles A., "Distribution in Latin America," in *Proceedings of the Boston Conference on Distribution,* Retail Trade Board, Boston Chamber of Commerce, 1959.

Michel, David, "Developments in the Structure of Distribution in France: A Moderate Degree of Concentration," *Journal of Retailing* (Summer, 1965), pp. 34ff.

Miller, Dudley L., "The Honorable Picnic: Doing Business in Japan," *Harvard Business Review* (November–December, 1961), pp. 79–86.

Miller, J. P., "Competition and Countervailing Power: Their Roles in the American Economy," in *American Economic Association Papers and Proceedings* (May, 1954), pp. 15–25.

Mintz, Sidney W., "The Role of the Middleman in the Internal Distribution System of a Caribbean Peasant Economy," in S. George

Walters et al. (eds.), *Readings in Marketing,* South-Western Publishing Company, Cincinnati, 1962, pp. 786–799.

MOLINARI, GIANFRANCO, "Latest Developments in Automatic Retailing in Europe," *Journal of Marketing* (October, 1964), pp. 5–9.

MOYER, REED, "The Structure of Markets in Developing Economies," *Business Topics* (Autumn, 1964), pp. 43–60.

NICHOLLS, WILLIAM H., "Domestic Trade in an Underdeveloped Country—Turkey," *The Journal of Political Economy* (December, 1951), pp. 463–480.

NORBY, JOHN C., "Consumers' Cooperatives in Norway," *Journal of Marketing* (April, 1952), pp. 423–434.

"The Overseas Boom in Door-to-door Selling," *Dun's Review and Modern Industry* (November, 1964), pp. 35ff.

PARR, C. M., "Why the Middleman?" *Journal of Business* (January, 1944), pp. 23–36.

PHELPS, D. MAYNARD, "Soviet Marketing—Stronger than We Think," *Harvard Business Review* (July, 1961), pp. 69–80.

——, "Opportunities and Responsibilities of the Franchised Automobile Dealer," *Journal of Marketing* (July, 1965), pp. 29–36.

PRESTON, LEE E., "Restrictive Distribution Arrangements: Economic Analysis and Public Policy Standards," *Law and Contemporary Problems,* Duke University School of Law, Durham, N.C. (Summer, 1965), pp. 506–529.

—— and S. E. SCHRAMM, JR., "Dual Distribution and Its Impact on Marketing Organization," *California Management Review* (Winter, 1965), pp. 59–70.

REVZAN, DAVID A., "Some Selected Trends in Wholesaling," in *Proceedings: Conference of Marketing Teachers from Far Western States,* University of California, Berkeley, Calif. (September, 1958), pp. 99–118.

RIDGEWAY, VALENTINE F., "Administration of Manufacturer-Dealer Systems," *Administrative Science Quarterly* (March, 1957), pp. 464–477.

ROBBINS, GEORGE W., "Notions about the Origins of Trading," in Charles J. Dirksen, Arthur Kroeger, and Lawrence C. Lockley (eds.), *Readings in Marketing,* Richard D. Irwin, Inc., Homewood, Ill., 1963, pp. 18–30.

SAMLI, A. COSKUN, "Wholesaling in an Economy of Scarcity: Turkey," *Journal of Marketing* (July, 1964), pp. 55–58.

SEGALL, MORRIS S., "Some Characteristics of Retail Competition in Canada," *Journal of Marketing* (July, 1955), pp. 62–65.

SHAUL, J. R. H., "Distributive Trades of Southern Rhodesia," *South African Journal of Economics* (June, 1953), pp. 186–193.

SHEPPARD, E. J., "Marketing Integration in Early Ohio," *Journal of Marketing* (October, 1954), pp. 166–168.

SHERBINI, A. A., "Marketing in the Industrialization of Underdeveloped Countries," *Journal of Marketing* (January, 1965), pp. 28–32.

SHYCON, HARVEY N., and RICHARD B. MAFFEI, "Simulation—Tool for Better Distribution," *Harvard Business Review* (November–December, 1960), pp. 66–75.

SIDDALL, WILLIAM R., "Wholesale-Retail Trade Ratios as Indices of Urban Centrality," *Economic Geography* (April, 1961), pp. 124–132.

SILBERMAN, CHARLES E., "The Revolutionists of Retailing," *Fortune* (April, 1962), pp. 99ff.

SMITH, CHARLES W., "Are You Paying Too Much for Distribution?" *Dun's Review and Modern Industry* (January, 1958), p. 42.

SMITH, PAUL E., and EUGENE J. KELLEY, "Competing Retail Systems: The Shopping Center and the Central Business District," *Journal of Retailing* (Spring, 1960), pp. 11–18.

SMITH, WENDELL R., "Product Differentiation and Market Segmentation as Alternative Marketing Strategies," *Journal of Marketing* (July, 1956), pp. 3–8.

"South African Retailing," *Economist* (Oct. 16, 1965), p. 318.

SPECTOR, SAMUEL I., "Retail Management in Israel," *Journal of Retailing* (Spring, 1959), pp. 85ff.

STASCH, STANLEY F., "The Stability of Channel Systems: Two Dynamic Models," in R. M. Haas (ed.), *Science, Technology, and Marketing,* American Marketing Association, Chicago, 1967, pp. 433–453.

STERN, LOUIS W., "Channel Control and Inter-organizational Management," in *Economic Growth, Competition, and World Markets,* American Marketing Association, Chicago, 1965, pp. 655–665.

STEWART, CHARLES F., "The Changing Middle East Market," *Journal of Marketing* (January, 1961), pp. 47–51.

STOCKING, G. W., and W. F. MUELLER, "Business Reciprocity and the Size of Firms," *Journal of Business* (April, 1957), pp. 73–95.

STRIDSBERG, ALBERT B., "Launching Your Product in Belgium," *Journal of Marketing* (January, 1962), pp. 1–5.

STURDIVANT, FREDERICK D., "Determinants of Vertical Integration in Channel Systems," in R. M. Haas (ed.), *Science, Technology, and Marketing,* American Marketing Association, Chicago, 1966, pp. 472–479.

"A Supermarket without a Store," *Business Week* (Jan. 11, 1964), pp. 100–102.

TALLMAN, GERALD B., and BRUCE BLOMSTROM, "Retail Innovations Challenge Manufacturers," *Harvard Business Review* (September–October, 1962), pp. 130–141.

TAYLOR, DONALD A., "Retailing in Brazil," *Journal of Marketing* (July, 1959), pp. 54–58.

TRACEY, M. B., "British Retail Institutions," *Journal of Retailing* (Summer, 1957), pp. 93ff.

VAILE, ROLAND S., "Changing Distribution Channels" (report of round table discussion), in *American Economic Association Papers and Proceedings* (March, 1939), pp. 104–108.

WADINAMBIARATCHI, GEORGE, "Channels of Distribution in Developing Economies," *The Business Quarterly* (Winter, 1965), pp. 74–82.

WALES, HUGH G., F. F. WINKLE, and C. BAK, "Marketing in South Africa," *Journal of Marketing* (October, 1963), pp. 42–47.

WALTERS, J. HART, JR., "Retailing in Poland: A First-hand Report," *Journal of Marketing* (April, 1964), pp. 16–21.

WARSHAW, MARTIN R., "Pricing to Gain Wholesalers' Selling Support," *Journal of Marketing* (July, 1962), pp. 50–54.

WASHINGTON, CANAS L., "Food Retailing Practices in Chile," *Journal of Retailing* (Fall, 1961), pp. 32–33.

WEIGAND, ROBERT E., "Department Stores in Japan," *Journal of Retailing* (Fall, 1963), pp. 31ff.

WELD, L. D. H., "Marketing Agencies between Manufacturer and Jobber," *American Journal of Economics* (August, 1917), pp. 571–99.

———, "Marketing Functions and Mercantile Organization," *American Economic Review* (June, 1917), pp. 306–318.

WESTFALL, RALPH, and HARPER W. BOYD, JR., "Marketing in India," *Journal of Marketing* (October, 1960), pp. 11–17.

WHITNEY, S. N., "Errors in the Concept of Countervailing Power," *Journal of Business* (October, 1953), pp. 238–253.

Government and International Agencies

Federal Trade Commission:

Report of the Federal Trade Commission on Distribution Methods and Costs (parts I–IV), 1944.

Economic Inquiry into Food Marketing, Part 1: Concentration and Integration in Retailing, Staff Report to the Federal Trade Commission, 1960.

———, *Part II: The Frozen Fruit, Juice and Vegetable Industry,* Staff Report to the Federal Trade Commission, 1962.

National Commission on Food Marketing:

Food from Farmer to Consumer, Report of the National Commission on Food Marketing, Superintendent of Documents, June, 1966. [See also the ten technical studies published by the Commission covering organization and competition in the livestock and meat industry (No. 1), poultry and egg industries (No. 2), dairy industry (No. 3), fruit and vegetable industry (No. 4), milling and baking industries (No. 5), grocery manufacturing (No. 6), and food retailing (No. 7); the structure of food manufacturing (No. 8), cost components of farm-retail price spreads for foods (No. 9), and special studies in food marketing (No. 10).]

Organization for European Economic Cooperation:

HENKSMEIER, H. K., *The Economic Performance of Self-service in Europe,* Paris, 1960.

JEFFERYS, JAMES B., et al., *Productivity in the Distributive Trade in Europe,* Paris, 1954.

Marketing Fruits and Vegetables in Europe, Project 249C, Paris, 1956.

Voluntary Chains in Europe: Structure, Organization, Results, Paris, 1961, mimeographed.

Small Business Administration:

CLEWETT, RICHARD M., "Checking Your Marketing Channels," *Management Aids for Small Manufacturers* (January, 1961).

VOLPP, LOUIS D., *Statistics and Maps for National Market Analysis,* Small Business Bibliography, No. 12, 1965.

U.S. Department of Commerce:

SEVIN, C. H., *Distribution Cost Analysis* (Economic Series 50), 1946.

———, *How Manufacturers Reduce Their Distribution Costs* (Economic Series 72), 1948.

U.S. House of Representatives:

The Impact upon Small Business of Dual Distribution and Related Vertical Integration, a report of Subcommittee No. 4 on Distribution Problems to the Select Committee on Small Business, 88th Cong., 1964.

Indexes

Name Index

Abbott, John C., 49
Alderson, Wroe, 62, 124, 134, 139, 142–144, 147
Alexander, Ralph S., 109, 125
Allvin, Paul E., 48, 55
Alton, A. J., 47
Artle, Roland, 133
Aspinwall, Leo, 136–138, 142, 145
Atlantic Refining Company, 75

Baker, Raymond W., 57
Balderston, Frederick, 134, 135
Baligh, Helmy H., 146, 147
Barger, Harold, 21
Bartsch, Nicholas, 54
Berg, Thomas L., 109, 125, 133
Berglund, S., 133
Boyd, Harper W., 45, 60
Breyer, Ralph F., 139
Brion, John M., 22
Brisco, Norris, A., 17
Brown Shoe Company, 74, 78
Bucklin, Louis P., 145–147
Bursk, Edward C., 122, 123

Carson, David, 60, 61
Cassady, Ralph, Jr., 19
Consolidated Foods Corporation, 80, 81
Corey, E. Raymond, 91
Cox, Reavis, 21, 140
Cundiff, Edward W., 42

David, Michel, 43, 48, 49
Day, Clive, 8, 10–12
deSalaberry, Louis, 48
Diamond, William T., 22
Dowd, Laurence P., 56, 57
Dunn, S. Watson, 47
Durant, Will, 9

Elgass, George A., 56, 57
England, W. B., 91, 92
Ewing, John S., 44

Galbraith, John K., 36
General Foods Corporation, 73, 74
General Motors Corporation, 78, 79
Gilchrist, F. W., 32
Gogol, V. I., 53
Goldman, Marshall I., 51–53
Green, Paul E., 134
Grether, Ewald T., 140

Hancock, Robert S., 67
Hirsch, Leon V., 58, 59
Hodges, Henry G., 92
Hoggatt, Austin, 134, 135
Hollander, Stanley C., 32, 35
Hotchkiss, George B., 10, 16

Jones, Fred M., 12, 13
Jones, Wylie L., 19

Lambert, Eugene W., Jr., 122
Lever Brothers Company, 74
Lewis, Edwin H., 20, 67, 99, 100, 117

McCammon, Bert C., Jr., 39
McInnes, William, 141
McNair, Malcolm P., 33
Marcus, Edward, 58
Marcus, Mildred R., 58
Martin, Miles W., 139
Mieschlag, Robert, 55

Palamountain, Joseph C., Jr., 40, 41
Pegram, Roger M., 126, 127
Phelps, D. Maynard, 52
Piercy, Ivan, 45
Preston, Lee E., 88
Proctor and Gamble Company, 74

Regan, William J., 37, 38
Richartz, Leon, 146, 147

Sandura Company, 76
Schramm, S. E., Jr., 88
Schwinn, Arnold, & Company, 77
Sealy Incorporated, 77
Sinclair Refining Company, 79
Snap-on Tools Corporation, 76
Stasch, Stanley F., 73
Sturdivant, Frederick D., 68, 69

Taylor, Donald A., 60
Tracey, M. B., 45

Vaile, Roland S., 140
Volpp, Louis D., 98

Walters, J. Hart, 53, 54
Weigand, Robert E., 57
Westfall, Ralph, 60
White Motor Company, 77
Wright, John S., 43

Zimmern, A., 9

Subject Index

Africa, Central, retailing in, 57, 58, 60

Agent middlemen, characteristics of, 13–15

  growth of, 27

  types of, 14, 15

Agents, manufacturers', 14, 27

  purchasing, 15, 27

  selling, 15, 27

Assemblers of farm products, 28

Auction company, 14

Australia, retailing in, 43, 44

Bayesian analysis in channel decisions, 133, 134

Branches, manufacturers' wholesale, 25, 26, 85

  growth of, 69

Brands, distributor (private), 103, 104

Broker, 14

Buyers, resident, 15, 27

Buying, by Federal government, 106, 107

  industrial, 104–106

Buying organizations, retail, 102

Chain stores, early, in U.S., 17, 18

  in Western Europe, 48

  (*See also* Retailers)

Channel decisions, evaluation of middlemen, 128, 129

  factors in, 115–128

    competitive practices, 118, 119

    legal restraints, 120, 121

    manufacturer's capability, 118

    market characteristics, 116, 117

    product line, 115, 116

  feedback in, 129, 130

  in marketing mix (strategy), 108, 109

  models for, 130–133, 146, 147

  procedures for, 130–133

  quantitative techniques for, 133–135

    Bayesian analysis, 133, 134

    simulation procedures, 134, 135

  selection of middlemen, 126–128

Channels of distribution, in Central Africa, 57, 58, 60, 61

  competition among, 4, 5

  conflicts within, 64–66

    caused by large-scale retailers, 65

    caused by manufacturers, 64, 66

    caused by wholesalers, 65

  control of, by Federal government, 73–81

    through integration, 68

    by manufacturers, 66, 67

  dynamics of, 5, 124, 125, 147, 148

  in Eastern Europe, 53, 54

  and economic development, 42–44

  efficiency of, 4, 72

  evolution of, 1, 2, 8

    in Europe, 9–11

    in U.S., 12–41

  feedback in, 129, 130

  functions performed, 3, 4

  in India, 58–60

  innovation in, 38–41, 124, 125

    related to political action, 40, 41

  institutional components of, 2, 4

  in Japan, 55–57

  manufacturer-consumer, 112

  manufacturer-retailer, 110, 111

  manufacturer-wholesaler, 112, 113

  in marketing strategy (mix), 5, 6

  nature of, 2, 3

  power relationships in, 63, 64

  purpose of, 2

  in Soviet Union, 51–53

  terminal points of, 3

  types of, 139

Channel investment, 122, 123

Channel transactions, routine, 124

"Characteristics of goods" theory, 136–138

Commission houses (merchants), 14, 28

  conflicts with producers, 65

Common Market, European, retailing in, 50, 51

  wholesaling in, 51

Cooperatives, consumer, 71, 72
  in Great Britain, 44
  in Soviet Union, 51, 52
  in Western Europe, 47
Countervailing power, 36

Department stores, buying organizations
    for, 102
  in Great Britain, 45
  in U.S., development of, 16, 17
    status of, 29, 30
  (*See also* Retailers)
Depot theory of distribution, 142, 145
Discount houses, characteristics of, 34
  in U.S., growth of, 32, 33, 39
  in Western Europe, 49, 50
Distributors, truck, 24, 25
  (*See also* Wholesalers)
Drop shippers, 24, 25
Dual distribution, 88–90

Exclusive distribution, legal aspects of,
    75–77
  territorial restrictions in, 76, 77

Factor [*see* Commission houses (mer-
    chants)]
Fair-trade laws, 41
Fairs, medieval, 10, 11
Feedback in channels, 129, 130
France, retailing in, 43, 47–49
Franchise systems, 67, 68
  legal aspects of, 77–79
Functions, allocation within the chan-
    nel, 110–114

Germany, retailing in, 48
  wholesaling in, 55
Great Britain, direct selling in, 46
  retailing in, 44–46

India, channels of distribution in, 58,
    59
Integration, vertical, 68, 69
Investment in customers, 122, 123
Italy, wholesaling in, 55

Japan, channels of distribution in, 55–57
Jobbers, definition, 13
  in 19th century America, 12, 13
  rack, 24
  (*See also* Wholesalers)
Joint opportunity, concept of, 67

Limited distribution [*see* Selective (lim-
    ited) distribution]

Mail-order houses, in Great Britain, 46
  in U.S., formation of, 17
    status of, 29
  (*See also* Retailers)
Marketing flows concept, 140, 141
Markets, medieval, 10, 11
  in Nigeria, 57
Market separation (gap) theory, 141,
    142
Merchants (*see* Retailers; Wholesalers)
Mergers, conglomerate, 73
  submarket concept, 74
  threat to competition, 73–75, 80
Middlemen, in Colonial America, 12
  early European, 9–10
  evaluation of, 128, 129
  evolution in U.S., 12–41
  feedback from, 129, 130
  medieval, 10, 11
  selection of, 126–128
  use of term, 3
  (*See also,* Agent middlemen; Retail-
      ers; Wholesalers)
Models, channel decision, 130–133, 146,
    147

National Industrial Conference Board, 126, 127

Negotiation process, 62, 63

Opportunity cost, 122

"Parallel-systems" theory, 137, 138
Poland, retailing in, 53, 54
Policies, distribution, 82–94
  dual distribution, 88–90
  general distribution, 85
  of manufacturers, 82–93
    direct to retailers, 84, 85
    selective (limited) distribution, 85–87
  nature of, 82, 83
  of wholesalers, 93–100
Postponement-speculation principle, 144–146
Purchasing (*see* Buying)

Reciprocity, corporate, in distribution policy, 90–93
  legal aspects of, 79–81
"Refusal-to-deal," 79
Retailer cooperatives, 70, 71, 102, 103
Retailers, in Colonial America, 16
  competition among, 38–41
  innovations by, 38, 39
  merchandise decisions of, 100, 101
  merchandise-service mix of, 37, 38
  in U.S., large-scale rise of, 16–18
  large-scale status of, 29–33
Retailing, in Australia, 44
  in Central Africa, 57, 58, 60
  in Eastern Europe, 53, 54
  in European Common Market, 50, 51
  in Great Britain, 44–46
  in India, 58, 60
  in Soviet Union, 51, 52
  in Western Europe, 43, 46–50
Robinson-Patman Act, 40

Selective (limited) distribution, 66, 67, 84–87
  customer selection in, 126–128
Simulation, channel flow, 72, 73
  procedures, 134, 135
Sorting concept, 142–144
Soviet Union, consumer cooperatives in, 51, 52
  retailing in, 51, 52
  wholesaling in, 52, 53
Supermarkets, 101
  operating results, 34
  in U.S., growth of, 30, 31, 39
  in Western Europe, 49

Technological distance, 143
Trade channel (*see* Channels of distribution)
Traders (*see* Middlemen)
Trading areas, wholesale, 96–100
Transformations, 144
Transvection concept, 139, 144
"Tying" arrangements, legal aspects of, 76, 78

Voluntary chains, 94–96
  economic bases for, 95
  in European Common Market, 50
  services to retailers, 95, 96
  in U.S., growth of, 18, 19, 40, 70
  in Western Europe, 47, 48

"Wheel of retailing" concept, 33–35
Wholesalers, cash-and-carry, 24
  in Colonial America, 12
  competition from retailers, 17, 18
  distribution policies of, 93–100
  grocery, operating expenses of, 114
  innovations among, 38, 39
  limited-service, 24, 25
  mail-order, 24
  merchant, new types of, 20, 21
  status of, in U.S., 21–24

Wholesalers, in 19th century America, 12, 13

trading areas of; 96–100

(*See also* Agent middlemen; Branches; Retailer cooperatives; Voluntary chains)

Wholesaling, in European Common Market, 51

grocery, 19, 20

in Japan, 55, 56

in Soviet Union, 52, 53

in Western Europe, 54, 55